Britain and Europe in a Troubled World

VERNON BOGDANOR

Yale UNIVERSITY PRESS

New Haven and London

The Henry L. Stimson Lectures at the Whitney and Betty
MacMillan Center for International for International and Area
Studies at Yale.

Yale University Press books may be purchased in quantity for
educational, business, or promotional use. For information, please
e-mail sales.press@yale.edu (U.S. office) or sales@yaleup.co.uk
(U.K. office).

Set in Minion type by IDS Infotech, Ltd.
Printed in Great Britain by TJ International Ltd, Padstow, Cornwall

ISBN 978-0-300-24561-5 (hardcover : alk. paper)
Library of Congress Control Number: 2020932736
A catalogue record for this book is available from the British
Library.

This paper meets the requirements of ANSI/NISO Z39.48-1992
(Permanence of Paper).

10 9 8 7 6 5 4 3 2 1

Contents

Acknowledgments

This book is based on a set of Stimson Lectures, delivered at Yale University in April 2019. I was invited to give them by Ian Shapiro, Sterling Professor of Political Science and Director of the MacMillan Center at Yale. I am deeply grateful to him, not only for honouring me with the invitation but for his wonderful hospitality and for the stimulus of his ideas and criticism. A number of other distinguished professors at Yale were generous enough to attend the lectures and to give me the benefit of their criticisms. I would like to thank, in particular, Professors Bruce Ackerman, Akhil Reed Amar, Paul Kennedy, and Joseph La Palombara. I count myself fortunate to have been a member, even if only for a short time, of such an invigorating society.

I have been fortunate also in that a number of other friends have been kind enough to criticise earlier versions of these lectures—Rudolf Adam, Chris Beauman, Gareth Cadwallader, Agata Gostynska-Jakubowska, Paul McIntyre, Luuk van Middelaar, Malcolm Murfett, Nancy Neville, Raymond Seitz, Sandy Sullivan, and Christopher Tugendhat. In addition, Tim Garton Ash and Madeleine Sumption were kind enough to respond to queries. I am also deeply grateful to Anthony Teasdale, co-editor of the invaluable 'Penguin Companion to European Union.' Not only has he read the manuscript with great care and made many constructive suggestions, most of which I have adopted; he has also given me the benefit over many years of his deep knowledge both of the European Union and of the Conservative party. But none of these kind friends should be implicated in my arguments or conclusions, much less my errors, which are entirely my responsibility.

I am grateful also to Elisha Cruz, Lourdes Haynes, Ozan Say, Carol Sequino, and Jennie Shamasna who helped to make my stay at Yale so very comfortable and enjoyable. Thanks also to William Frucht, Philip King, and Karen Olson, who made publishing with Yale University Press so pleasant an experience

But my greatest debt is to my wife, Sonia, who not only read an early draft, making valuable criticisms, but also encouraged and sustained me throughout.

Chronology

1950   Schuman Declaration proposes that France and
        Germany pool their coal and steel production.
1951   Treaty of Paris establishes the Coal and Steel
        Community.
1955   Messina Conference of the six members of the Coal
        and Steel Community reaches agreement on a
        customs union.
1957   Treaty of Rome establishes European Communities,
        to come into force in 1958.
1959   European Free Trade Association is set up
        comprising seven member states not in the European
        Communities, including Britain.
1960   April. Blue Streak nuclear missile programme
        abandoned, replaced by U.S.-led Skybolt.
1960   May. Breakdown of summit conference.
1961   Prime Minister Harold Macmillan opens negotiations
        on British entry into the European Communities.
1962   September. Labour Party leader Hugh Gaitskell
        opposes British entry into the European Communities.
1962   December. U.S. government cancels Skybolt and
        replaces it with Polaris missiles for use on British
        submarines as part of a NATO multilateral force.

1963   President Charles de Gaulle of France vetoes British
        application.

1964   General election. Labour Party returns to power
        under Harold Wilson.

1967   Wilson announces application to join European
        Community. Vetoed later that year by de Gaulle.

1970   General election. Conservatives return to power
        under Edward Heath, who renews the application to
        join European Community.

1971   President Georges Pompidou, successor to de Gaulle,
        agrees to British application.

1972   Parliament passes European Communities Act
        providing for entry in 1973.

1974   General election. Labour returns to power under
        Harold Wilson. Renegotiation of terms of entry.

1975   Referendum on the renegotiated terms. Two-to-one
        majority for remaining in the Community.

1979   European Monetary System introduced. Britain does
        not join. General election. Conservatives return to
        power under Margaret Thatcher.

1984   Fontainebleau summit agrees to a rebate on British
        budgetary contribution.

1986   Single European Act, amending Treaty of Rome, is
        signed and ratified by member governments and
        parliaments.

1988   Margaret Thatcher's Bruges lecture stressing
        the role of the member states in constructing
        Europe.

1990   Britain joins exchange rate mechanism of European
        Monetary System. John Major succeeds Margaret
        Thatcher as Conservative prime minister.

1992   Maastricht treaty creates the European Union and
        provides for a common currency, the euro, but with a

British opt-out. Britain leaves exchange rate mechanism and floats the pound.

1993   Parliament ratifies Maastricht treaty.

1997   General election. Labour returns to power under Tony Blair.

2004   Enlargement of the European Union to include the former Communist states of central and eastern Europe.

2007   Gordon Brown succeeds Blair as Labour prime minister. Lisbon treaty, amending previous treaties, is signed and ratified, entering into force in 2009.

2010   General election. Conservative/Liberal Democrat coalition is formed under the Conservative leader, David Cameron. Angela Merkel's Bruges lecture emphasises the 'Union method' of co-ordinated action by national governments in the construction of Europe.

2013   David Cameron promises to renegotiate British membership and put the outcome to referendum.

2015   General election. Conservatives win small overall majority. David Cameron continues as prime minister, but of single-party government.

2016   Referendum outcome is 52 percent to 48 percent against remaining in the European Union. Cameron resigns as prime minister, to be succeeded by Theresa May.

2017   British government invokes Article 50, giving notice of its intention to leave the European Union in 2019.

2017   General election. Conservatives lose overall majority.

2018   Parliament passes European Union Withdrawal Act, repealing the European Communities Act of 1972.

2019   Theresa May resigns as prime minister, having failed to secure parliamentary approval for the withdrawal agreement negotiated with the European Union. Replaced by Boris Johnson.

2019   General election. Conservatives secure overall majority by eighty seats and proceed to implement the withdrawal agreement.

2020   European Union (Withdrawal Agreement) Act receives royal assent and, on 31 January, Great Britain leaves the European Union.

Britain and Europe in a Troubled World

1

'Reserve, but Proud Reserve'
Britain Detached from Europe

Britain's relationship with the continent of Europe has long been an uneasy one. My goal is to cast light not only on this very important topic, but also on some fundamental problems of modern politics—the grand themes of nationalism and internationalism, sovereignty and identity, and, perhaps most fundamental of all, the question of whether a nation can or should seek to escape from its past, a problem of particular significance to a country such as Britain, with its long evolutionary and on the whole peaceful history. It is perhaps worth stressing the deep historic origins of the British system of government. The monarchy can trace its beginnings to the seventh century A.D., while Parliament has its origins in mediaeval times, many centuries before the United States was conceived. Does that history remain an inspiration, or has it become instead a constraint, preventing Britain from adjusting effectively to the modern world?

The working out of these themes in Europe is of as much importance to Americans as it is to Europeans. Indeed, Henry Stimson was himself concerned as Franklin D. Roosevelt's war secretary with the postwar reconstruction of Europe, although the main problems that he faced, both as secretary of state under Herbert Hoover and secretary of war under Roosevelt and Harry Truman, were concerned with Asia and in particular Japan. He was, however, most definitely an internationalist; and, during his lifetime, it became clear that the United States could not but be concerned with what was happening in Europe.

The United States has indeed been deeply involved in European politics for much of the twentieth century. Perhaps Europe first impinged upon the United States at the beginning of that century. In 1911, there was a crisis in Europe that could have led to war when Germany sought to contest French claims to a sphere of interest in Morocco, which was to become a French protectorate in 1912. Britain, in accordance with the entente, took the side of France. After the crisis had been resolved, America's former president Theodore Roosevelt told the German ambassador that if Germany had overrun France, the United States would not have remained neutral. The ambassador answered that this seemed contrary to the Monroe Doctrine. Roosevelt replied in the following way: 'As long as England succeeds in keeping up the "balance of power" in Europe, not only in principle, but in reality, well and good; should she however for some reason or other fail in doing so, the United States would be obliged to step in at least temporarily, in order to re-establish the balance of power in Europe, never mind against which country. . . . In fact we ourselves are becoming, owing to our strength and geographical position, more and more the balance of power on the whole globe.'[1]

That was an astonishing prediction of the course of twentieth-century history. Twice indeed during that century, Americans felt that they were compelled, as Theodore Roosevelt had intuited, to 'step in' to protect the balance of power in Europe and resist German attempts to become the dominant power on the Continent. Twice, if the world wars had been confined to European powers, Germany might well have won. The key factors in both world wars were the entry into them of the United States and the fact that the large Eurasian land mass of Russia, which was only partially a European power, was brought into play against Germany. Americans might have thought that an obscure Balkan quarrel following the assassination of the heir to the Austrian throne at Sarajevo in 1914, or the quarrel between Germany and Poland in 1939 over the city of Danzig, had nothing to do with them. They would have been wrong. Following the end of World War I, in September 1919, President Woodrow Wilson, in a speech at Pueblo, Colorado— his last speech before he was disabled by a stroke—spoke of the Americans who had sacrificed their lives to create a better Europe and a better world. He paid tribute to 'the serried ranks of those boys in khaki, not only these boys who came home, but those dear ghosts that still deploy upon the fields of France.' He wanted to speak for 'the next generation' who were his clients, and said that he intended to redeem his pledge that 'They shall not be sent upon a similar errand.' In 1966, when President Charles de Gaulle of France sought a more independent stance in relation to NATO, he asked the United States to remove its men and bases from French territory. President Lyndon Johnson asked whether the American cemeteries containing the graves of some 60,000 American soldiers should be removed as well. There is no reason to believe that what happens in Europe today might not also impinge upon Americans. It is of course to be hoped that Europe's problems, by contrast with the past, are resolved peacefully. Indeed the main motivation behind the construction of the European Union was the desire to prevent future wars by overcoming the forces of nationalism which had caused them.

The European Union was and remains essentially a peace project. The history of Europe since 1914 falls neatly into two contrasting periods. Between the wars, politics on the continent was marked by turbulence and crisis, but for nearly seventy-five years, its western half has known political stability and high rates of economic growth. That is in large part due to the post-war recognition of collective security and interdependence in a continent that had suffered badly in the past from their absence.

The book from which I quoted Theodore Roosevelt's comment on the balance of power has as its title *The Last European War*. That is the description the author gives to the Second World War, since he believes it to be the last war fought to prevent one European power from dominating the others. The end of the Cold War makes it highly unlikely that a purely European power will ever again seek to dominate the Continent; and of course no European power can hope to match the United States, a superpower. In the Second World War, however, Hitler's attempt to dominate Europe nearly succeeded. Had it done so, there would have been a united Europe, but it would not have been united in freedom. When, in 1940, the British government decided to continue the fight against Hitler against seemingly impossible odds, Winston Churchill said that Britain was fighting 'by ourselves alone, but not for ourselves alone.' The British were fighting for Europe as well as for Britain. Churchill's aim was to liberate Europe. Once that had been achieved, European leaders had to decide how such catastrophes could be avoided in the future. They came to the view that Nazism and Fascism were but extreme examples of nationalism, and that Europe would not know peace until nationalism had been transcended.

At the beginning of the twentieth century, however, the force of nationalism had appeared as an essential concomitant of self-government, and therefore of democracy. The ideal of self-determination was founded on the nineteenth-century liberal view that humanity was naturally divided into nations and that every nation should have its own state. It was a doctrine championed with great enthusiasm by Woodrow Wilson. In Europe, the twentieth-century ideal of self-determination was perhaps well symbolised by Józef Piłsudski, the Polish leader between the wars who tried, though without success, to create a multinational Polish state in which not only Poles but also minorities—Jews, Ukrainians, Lithuanians, and Germans— would feel comfortable. Piłsudski had begun as a socialist, but when he led the movement for Polish independence, and his former socialist comrades approached him for support, he rejected them with the following words: 'Comrades,' he said, 'I rode on the red-painted tramcar of socialism as far as the stop called Independence, but there I alighted.' And he then added, 'You are free to drive on to the terminus if you can, but please address me as "Sir"!'[2]

Piłsudski's journey in a sense symbolises the twentieth century. In the nineteenth century, Karl Marx had predicted a future based on class war and revolution. Instead, the twentieth century was one in which the classes collaborated and wars were fought in Europe between multinational empires and independent nation-states. After the fall of communism, at the end of the twentieth century, popular nationalism, long suppressed by communist regimes, succeeded in destroying the Russian Empire, created by the Czars and extended by Stalin, as well as the two multinational states created in 1919 by the treaties which ended the First World War, Czechoslovakia and Yugoslavia. The legacy of Woodrow Wilson has outlasted that of Lenin.

In the nineteenth century, most liberals welcomed the advance of nationalism, which they associated with government by consent. For consent, so it seemed, was most easily conferred within a national community. The Italian liberal Giuseppe Mazzini considered nationalism an analogue on the political level to individual freedom. Mazzini had hoped to see a Europe of independent nation-states, freely cooperating together for the good of their peoples. Individual and collective self-determination were believed to be not only compatible but indeed complementary. It was for this reason that liberals supported nationalism against its enemies, whether those enemies were clerical, reactionary, or monarchical. In Britain, it was the struggle for Italian unity and self-determination, the Risorgimento, which persuaded Gladstone to switch from the Conservatives to the Liberal Party. In a speech at London's Guildhall on 9 November 1914, three months after Britain had gone to war, another Liberal prime minister, H. H. Asquith, declared that one of Britain's war aims was to ensure that 'the rights of the smaller nationalities of Europe are placed upon an unassailable foundation.' He was of course thinking of Serbia and of Belgium. But those sensitive to Britain's native hypocrisies might note that when, at the end of the war, one particular small nationality on its very own doorstep—the Irish—sought to secure these very rights by voting for the separatist Sinn Fein party in 1918, which refused to recognise Westminster and set up a separate parliament in Dublin, the response of the British government, far from ensuring that Ireland's rights were 'placed upon an unassailable foundation,' was to refuse to recognise the Dublin parliament and to attempt to put down Sinn Fein by force.

Men such as Gladstone and Asquith could not, of course, foresee that the generous impulses behind the Risorgimento would eventually lead to a Fascist regime in Italy led by Mussolini, who was to prove the model for Hitler. And perhaps Fascism and National Socialism, behind all of their rhetorical rodomontade, were really nothing more than labels for radical nationalism carried to extremes.

The twentieth century has, then, been inhospitable to the hopes of liberal nationalists such as Mazzini; and, by contrast with their nineteenth-century predecessors, twentieth-century liberals see nationalism as an enemy rather than a friend. In 1918, Woodrow Wilson's secretary of state, Robert Lansing, declared with some prescience that the phrase *self-determination* was 'loaded with dynamite. It will raise hopes that can never be realised. It will, I fear, cost thousands of lives. In the end it is bound to be discredited, to be called the dream of an idealist.'³ And the principle of self-determination was to be used by Hitler to justify his annexation of Austria and the German-speaking areas of Czechoslovakia in 1938. So, while the aim of nineteenth-century liberals was to give effect to nationalism, their successors in the latter half of the twentieth century have sought to transcend it.

The movement to unite Europe after 1945 was an attempt to constrain the force of nationalism, a force which, so it was believed, had been responsible for the ruinous wars which had ravaged the Continent. It was an attempt to replace an international system through which sovereign states somehow adjusted their claims against each other so as to preserve a balance of power, with a system in which these claims could be adjusted within a single framework, that of European unity. It was an attempt, as it were, to internalise conflict, so rendering it peaceful. It also had a geopolitical significance. For Europeans had come to realise that they could not preserve the balance of power entirely by themselves. They needed, as Theodore Roosevelt had foreseen, to call in the aid of the United States. The danger for Europeans, then, was that they would become subordinated to the United States, that decisions affecting Europe's future would be made on its behalf by Americans. The only way in which that dependence could be avoided would be if Europe were to unite. The idea of European unity stemmed from a sense of weakness, not of strength, a realisation that the destiny of Europe after two world wars was coming to depend not only upon the Continent's own efforts but upon the dispositions of extra-European powers. The idea of the balance of power, therefore, should, in the minds of Europe's founding fathers, be superseded by a new idea, the idea of European unity, an idea championed by idealists of all sorts, and particularly by those who had been prominent in the resistance.

Europe, however, had not been united since the end of the Roman Empire. Many since then had tried to unite Europe by conquest—most recently Napoleon and Hitler. Would it be possible to achieve this unity peacefully and democratically? That was the problem faced by the founding fathers of the movement for European unity. They found the answer by not confronting the issue directly. In the words of the Schuman Declaration, named after the French foreign minister Robert Schuman: 'Europe will not be made all at once or according to a single plan. It will be built through concrete achievements which first create a de facto solidarity.' The founding fathers appreciated that any direct attempt to construct a federal Europe would not succeed. Instead, Europe had to be built step by step, beginning with economic cooperation.

If I were to say that 9 May 1950 is one of the most important dates in postwar European history, perhaps *the* most important date in postwar European history, I suspect that most of my readers would not have the faintest idea what I was talking about. That was the date of the Schuman Declaration, which gave rise to the first steps towards European unity, the European Coal and Steel Community, established by the Treaty of Paris in 1951. 'Every decade that passes,' one commentator has written, 'confirms this event as one of the landmarks of the century. The implications go well beyond Europe.'[4] Robert Schuman had been born in Luxembourg but spent much of his early life in the border area of Lorraine, which was a part of Germany until 1919, having been conquered by Bismarck in his war against France in 1870. Schuman had in fact been conscripted to fight for Germany in 1914 but had been rejected on health grounds. In the Second World War, he had been a member of the French resistance. So he had been a German citizen before becoming a French citizen at the age of thirty-two. He regarded himself as a Franco-German.

Schuman himself was not, however, the prime mover of the project. That honour belongs to Jean Monnet, a businessman and international civil servant. Never elected to any public office, Monnet wielded greater influence in the twentieth century than almost all elected politicians. He is generally regarded as the father of European unity and the first statesman of interdependence.[5] On 5 August 1943, he had told the French National Liberation Committee, 'There will be no peace in Europe, if the states are reconstituted on the basis of national sovereignty. . . . The countries of Europe are too small to guarantee their peoples the necessary prosperity and social development. The European states must constitute themselves into a federation.' It was Monnet who wrote the Schuman Declaration. The Schuman Plan might well have been called the Monnet Plan.

The movement for unity began with regulation of the production of coal and steel under a supranational authority, the European Coal and Steel Community. It continued with the Treaty of Rome in 1957, establishing the European Communities, sometimes called the Common Market, which became a single European Community in 1967, and then with the Treaty of Maastricht in 1992 establishing the European Union and providing for a common European currency, the euro.

The Schuman plan, which formed the basis of the Coal and Steel Community, was intended as the answer to a practical problem, that of reintegrating West Germany into the economic life of western Europe so as to ensure the revival of the war-ravaged continent. Germany in the late 1940s was not only defeated but also divided, and that, perhaps, made it easier to integrate West Germany with France. For the French, however, the problem was how they could be persuaded to accept the economic revival of their ancient enemy, a revival which might also lead to the revival of Germany's war-making power. Monnet's answer to the problem was to alter the context within which it was posed, and, by creating supranational institutions, to replace national rivalry with international cooperation.

The Schuman Plan was based on a mixture of fear and hope. The fear was that the industrial might of Germany, and particularly its strength in the production of coal and steel, might provide the basis for a revival of the country's military strength, leading to German rearmament and renewed German aggression. For coal and steel were the keys not only to economic power but also to military power. Monnet and Schuman did not believe that this fear could be addressed through the permanent repression of Germany. That, in their view, had been the mistake of French policy between the wars. The hope, therefore, was that peace could be secured through a policy of reconciliation. But how could this be achieved? The answer lies in the Schuman Declaration.

> The coming together of the nations of Europe requires the elimination of the age-old opposition of France and Germany. Any action taken must in the first place concern these two countries.
>
> With this aim in view, the French Government proposes that action be taken immediately on one limited but decisive point.
>
> It proposes that French and German production of coal and steel as a whole be placed under a common High Authority, whose decisions would be binding, within the framework of an organisation open to the participation of the other countries of Europe.

The hope was to turn coal and steel into weapons of peace, and so undermine the basis of Franco-German antagonism. The movement for European unity was, from the beginning, fundamentally a peace project designed to integrate the new Germany into Europe. As Edward Heath, the prime minister who took Britain into the European Community, told the House of Commons in April 1975, the European Communities had been 'founded for a political purpose. . . . It was not a federal, but a political purpose, the political purpose was . . . to absorb the new Germany into the structure of the European family, and economic means were adopted for that very political purpose.'[6] The European Coal and Steel Community was devised during the period of the Cold War, when Europe was divided. But the movement to integrate Europe was not intended to ratify the division of the Continent. 'It is not our task or wish to draw frontier lines', insisted Churchill at the Albert Hall on 14 May 1947, 'but rather to smooth them away. Our aim is to bring about the unity of all nations of all Europe.'

A united Germany firmly anchored in Europe would be, for the Russians as well, the best assurance that there would be no revival of German nationalism. 'The whole purpose', Churchill declared in his Albert Hall speech, 'of a united democratic Europe is to give definite guarantees against aggression. . . . The creation of a healthy and contented Europe is the first and truest interest of the Soviet Union. We had therefore hoped that all sincere efforts to promote European agreement and stability would receive, as they deserve, the sympathy and support of Russia.' Speaking at Brussels in February 1949, Churchill insisted, 'The Europe we seek to unite is *all* Europe.' But that was a dream not to be realised until the twenty-first century.

The immediate aim, then, was economic. But the ultimate aim was political—nothing less than the unity of Europe. To continue with the words of the Declaration:

The pooling of coal and steel production should
immediately provide for the setting up of common
foundations for economic development as a first
step in the federation of Europe.

This pooling of coal and steel production was not an end in
itself, but the beginning of a much wider policy having as its
eventual aim a European federation.

Before making his Declaration, Schuman had consulted
the German chancellor, Konrad Adenauer. The new Federal
Republic of Germany had been established in 1949. It comprised
only West Germany—for Germany was not to be reunified
until 1990, and the eastern part remained separate as the German Democratic Republic, under Communist rule. Adenauer,
West Germany's first postwar chancellor, was, like Schuman, a
Christian Democrat. His aim was to anchor West Germany
firmly into the western alliance, so he naturally grabbed at the
opportunity offered by the Schuman Plan.

What mechanism did the Schuman Plan propose? Schuman proposed that the coal and steel production of France and
Germany be placed under a common governing body called
the High Authority. That High Authority was to be a transnational body. Its members would be appointed by the member
states, but they were not to be representatives of the member
states. They were instead to represent a common European
interest, an interest which transcended the interests of the
separate member states. They were to embody a European, not
a national perspective.

At the press conference at which the Plan was launched,
one journalist asked Schuman whether this was not a leap into
the unknown. Schuman replied that it was indeed a leap into
the unknown. It was just ten years since the Germans had conquered Paris, and five years almost to the day since the defeat

of Nazi Germany. The Schuman Plan would, it was hoped, make war between France and Germany impossible. It would become, in Schuman's words, 'not only unthinkable but materially impossible.' France and Germany would, so a British diplomat commented, be 'in an embrace so close that neither could draw back far enough to hit the other.'[7] The Schuman Plan marked the birth of European unity. The Coal and Steel Community, like the European Union, had a Council of Ministers, a Court of Justice, and a Common Assembly—a European Parliament in embryo—though the Common Assembly, unlike the European Parliament today, was not directly elected but appointed by members of the various national parliaments, and it had only supervisory powers. Today's European Parliament of course enjoys much wider powers. The High Authority was the European Commission in embryo.

Since 1985, the date of the Schuman Plan, 9 May, has been known on the Continent as Europe Day, and sometimes as Schuman Day. There is apparently a move by Catholics to beatify Schuman—but it appears that the Catholic Church demands evidence of a miracle before that can occur. Some might perhaps say that the creation of the European Coal and Steel Community, just a few years after the end of the war, was such a miracle. Others might argue that the continued survival of the European Union has been a miracle. But the Catholic Church is not yet convinced!

If, as Schuman hoped, a European federation was eventually to be achieved, then the Coal and Steel Community would have to be open to all European democracies. In the event, the founding nations were France, Germany, Italy, and the Benelux countries—Belgium, Luxembourg, and the Netherlands. These were also the six founding nations of the European Communities, established by the Treaty of Rome in 1957. Britain never joined the Coal and Steel Community, and did not join the

European Community until 1973, after two previous attempts to join had been vetoed by the president of France, Charles de Gaulle. After Brexit, the European Union, successor to the Coal and Steel Community and the European Community, will have twenty-seven members; almost every other country in Europe belongs. The main exceptions are the countries of the western Balkans. There are currently five candidate members: Albania; the former Yugoslav republics of Macedonia (now called the Republic of North Macedonia), Montenegro, and Serbia; and Turkey. Bosnia and Kosovo, which did not become independent until 2008, may also become candidate members.

But the formative steps were taken in the 1950s. Dean Acheson, United States secretary of state from 1949 to 1953, called his memoir of the period *Present at the Creation*. It was a good title. For these were the years in which new relationships were being formed, relationships which were long to survive. Until the late 1950s, the countries of Europe had a great deal of freedom of manoeuvre, Britain particularly so, owing to the great prestige which the nation enjoyed after the war. Indeed, in the early postwar years, the leaders on the Continent would have happily accepted British leadership in the movement for European unity. After the 1950s, however, relationships were to become frozen, and it would prove very difficult to alter them. 'I believe,' a former British ambassador to the United States presciently declared in 1954, 'that history has given us a period within which to work out our problems. The period began with the end of the Second World War and may last as long as the working lifetime of my generation. It will not be longer; it may well be shorter—the whole period, whatever its duration may turn out to be, is crucial: what we do or fail to do in it will be decisive. After it there will be no second chance.'[8] He was right. Because Britain did not join the European Community until fifteen years after it was formed, the British had no voice in the institutional structure or the economic arrangements agreed upon by the founding members. Britain had to accept rules and institutions drawn up by others. It was to prove a serious handicap.

Britain, then, did not become a member of the Coal and Steel Community. At the time the idea was put forward, the country was governed by a Labour administration, which by 1950 had nationalised the coal industry and was in the process of nationalising the steel industry. How could these nationalised industries be integrated with a European authority predicated on the basis of private ownership? The government, moreover, was a firm believer in Keynesian economics. That required national control of the economy so that counter-cyclical measures could be introduced to maintain full employment. To cede control to the High Authority meant that this authority could insist on the closure of mines or steelworks in Britain. That was unacceptable. Labour's deputy prime minister, Herbert Morrison, said of the Schuman plan: 'It's no good. We cannot do it. The Durham miners won't wear it.'[9] Speaking for the Conservative opposition, the future prime minister Harold Macmillan, remembering the very high level of unemployment in Stockton, his constituency in the north of England in the years between the wars, said: 'One thing is certain. And we may as well face it. Our people are not going to hand over to any supranational authority the right to close down our pits or steelworks. We will allow no supranational authority to put large masses of our people out of work in Durham, in the Midlands, in South Wales, or in Scotland.'[10]

And, above all, there was the wider fear concerning the final destination of the European movement—a European federation. One Foreign Office official declared that 'British participation is likely to involve us in Europe beyond the point of no return, whether the plan involves some form of immediate

Federation in Europe or whether it is "the first step in the federation of Europe" as the French statement puts it or whether it is merely a species of European cartel.' Another official declared, 'To contemplate, even in principle, an agreement to pool the British coal and steel industries with those of other West European countries, and make their operations subject to the decisions of an independent European authority which are binding on Her Majesty's Government, would imply a readiness to accept a surrender of sovereignty in a matter of vital national interest which would carry us well beyond that point. The decision which the French are now summoning us to take is, in fact, the decision whether or not we are to bind ourselves irrevocably to the European community.'[11] Most leading Conservatives shared this view. Anthony Eden, speaking as foreign secretary at Columbia University in January 1952, a time when the American government was eager that Britain become part of a European political unit, told his American audience:

> If you drive a nation to adopt procedures which run counter to its instincts, you weaken and may destroy the motive force of its action. . . . You will realize that I am speaking of the frequent suggestions that the United Kingdom should join a federation on the continent of Europe. This is something which we know, in our bones, we cannot do.[12]

Eden, one of the ablest of twentieth-century British foreign secretaries, also said that membership of a European federation would violate 'the unalterable marrow' of the British nation. British resistance to joining a European federation was not something that could be overcome by argument, by an assessment of costs and benefits; it was an instinctive hostility, something which we knew 'in our bones' we could never join.

There was, finally some scepticism over whether such a bold scheme would ever come to fruition. Emanuel Shinwell, the defence secretary, declared, 'Don't buy this pig while it's still in the poke.'[13] A Foreign Office official told his minister: 'We should not get committed. . . . The Franco-German talks would inevitably break down sooner or later, and . . . we would then have the chance of coming in as *deus ex machina* with a solution of our own.'[14]

Absurd though that appears with hindsight, we must remember that French politics at the time was highly unstable, with governments lasting on average for around nine months. Just two weeks after Schuman made his speech, the French minister of finance told the chancellor of the Exchequer that he himself was sceptical—and that two former foreign ministers were also sceptical.[15] The Communists and the Gaullists, who saw it as an infringement of French sovereignty, were both hostile. Further, it was not possible so soon after the war to be confident that democracy on the Continent was entirely secure. Germany and Italy had only just reestablished democratic institutions, and there were large Communist parties both in Italy and in France. It was natural, therefore, for the government to think that perhaps the relationship with the Continent was not as important as other relationships. So Britain did not join. The 9th of May, the anniversary of the Schuman declaration, has always been ignored in Britain.

Britain's failure to join the Coal and Steel Community was a crucial turning point in European history. Until then, it had been assumed that Britain had a veto on European integration. David Bruce, an American diplomat responsible for the administration of the Marshall Plan, put forward three propositions in April 1950. The first was that 'there will be no real European integration without whole-hearted participation by the United Kingdom.' The second was that 'the United Kingdom will not whole-heartedly participate'; and so the third proposition was 'ergo, there will be no purely European integration.' That judgment was shared by British officials, one of whom had made the arrogant comment in 1948, 'If the United Kingdom does not lead the movement it will not occur. For no other country in Europe has the moral authority and the organising capacity.'[16] But the success of the Community proved to the leaders of the Continental powers that they could build a united Europe without British leadership or participation. The European Coal and Steel Community 'entrenched a Franco-German leadership in Europe into which the UK . . . has never been able to penetrate.'[17] Britain, therefore, was not present at the creation. And even after joining, the British remained ambivalent about a Continental commitment. Robert Schuman had declared that the nations of Europe shared a 'common European destiny.' Britain was always ambivalent about whether in fact it shared that destiny, or whether it was, quite simply, a different sort of country.

That ambivalence is well exemplified in the career of Britain's greatest twentieth-century statesman, Winston Churchill. He had been one of the first supporters of a united Europe, but he could not make up his mind as to whether Britain ought to be a part of it.

In the postwar years, Churchill's involvement in the European cause came about, so it seems, in a curious way. He had been defeated in the general election of 1945, and just over a year after the end of the war, on 19 September 1946, was due to make a speech at Zurich University. He was apparently in a grumpy mood before the speech. His son-in-law, the future Conservative minister Duncan Sandys, asked him why. Churchill replied that he was due to make a speech comparing the British parliamentary system and the Swiss cantonal system of government. 'But,' Sandys objected, 'you know nothing about it.' 'That is why I am so irritable,' the great man replied. Sandys suggested that instead of comparative government, Churchill should instead speak on the question they had been discussing that very evening at dinner—the future of Europe. That, it is said, was how the Zurich speech came to be born. It is a good story. It may even be true.

Churchill began his speech by stressing the ravages of a Europe still torn by war, and the danger that the Dark Ages, threatened by the Nazis 'in all their cruelty and squalor,' 'may still return.' 'When the Nazi power was broken, I asked myself what was the best advice I could give my fellow citizens in our ravaged and exhausted Continent. My counsel to Europe can be given in a single word: Unite!' There was, he declared, 'a remedy which, if it were generally and spontaneously adopted, would as if by a miracle transform the whole scene and would in a few years make all Europe, or the greater part of it, as free and happy as Switzerland is today.' That remedy was 'to recreate the European family, or as much of it as we can, and provide it with a structure under which it can dwell in peace, in safety, and in freedom. We must,' he insisted, 'build a kind of United States of Europe.' It is worth emphasising that he said 'a *kind* of United States of Europe.' Europe would not seek to imitate the United States but would discover its own, European method of achieving union. Many quote the words of the preamble to the Treaty of Rome, and embodied in later treaties, that the fundamental aim of the European movement is 'ever closer union.' But they do not quote the remainder of the phrase, 'ever closer union among the peoples of Europe.' That, perhaps, entails something very different from a United States of Europe.

Churchill then went on to say that a united Europe 'could give a sense of enlarged patriotism and common citizenship' to Europeans. He continued, 'I am now going to say something that will astonish you. The first step in the recreation of the

European family must be a partnership between France and Germany. . . . There can be no revival of Europe without a spiritually great France and a spiritually great Germany.' That was certainly a bold thing to say just sixteen months after the defeat of Nazi Germany.

The Zurich speech was by no means the first occasion on which Churchill had called for European unity. It had indeed been a persistent theme. In an article in *The Saturday Evening Post* in 1930, he had declared that 'the conception of a United States of Europe is right. Every step taken to that end which appeases the obsolete hatreds and vanished oppressions, which makes easier the traffic and reciprocal services of Europe, which encourages nations to lay aside their precautionary panoply, is good in itself.'

But he then went on to add, in words that prefigured his postwar policies, 'But we have our own dream and our own task; we are with Europe, but not of it. We are linked but not compromised.'[18] Then, with great prescience, a few days after Alamein in 1942, the first major British victory against Germany in the war, he wrote to his foreign secretary, Anthony Eden, with his views on the postwar world. 'I must admit that thoughts rest primarily in Europe—the revival of the glory of Europe, the parent continent of the modern nations and of civilisation.' He went on to say, 'Hard as it is to say now, I look forward to a United States of Europe in which the barriers between the nations will be greatly minimized and unrestricted travel will be possible.'[19]

In his Zurich speech, Churchill said that Britain must be among 'the friends and sponsors of the new Europe.' He did not say that Britain should actually be part of it, though in other speeches in the late 1940s he did explicitly suggest that Britain should become a part of the new European movement, indeed that the British should lead it. Nevertheless, his Conservative government, which was returned to power in 1951, adopted a policy of detachment hardly distinguishable from that of its Labour predecessor. Britain made no moves to join the Coal and Steel Community, and although Churchill supported the scheme in the European Defence Community for a European army, he did not believe that Britain should be part of that either. In opposition, Churchill had put forward the idea of a European army, but as prime minister in 1952 he declared, 'I really meant it for them [the Continental powers] and not for us.'[20] By the end of Churchill's premiership in 1955, Britain was in the position which it was so long to occupy of being outside the mainstream of European development.

Churchill's basic worry about involvement in Europe was that it would weaken the connection with the Commonwealth— or, as he preferred to call it, the Empire. When Britain sought for the first time—unsuccessfully, as it turned out—to join the European Communities, as the European Union then was, in 1961, under Harold Macmillan, Churchill was in retirement. And very uncharacteristically for him, he could not make up his mind whether Britain should join.

In a letter to the chair of his Conservative constituency party, he said:

> For many years I have believed that measures to promote European unity were ultimately essential to the well-being of the West. In a speech at Zurich in 1946 I urged the creation of the European Family, and I am sometimes given credit for stimulating the ideals of European unity which led to the formation of the economic and the other two communities. In the aftermath of the Second World War, the key to these endeavours lay in partnership between France and Germany. At that time this happy outcome seemed a fantasy, but it is now accomplished, and

France and West Germany are more intimately linked than they have ever been before in their history. They together with Italy, Belgium, Holland and Luxembourg, are welding themselves into an organic whole, stronger and more dynamic than the sum of its parts.

We might well play a great part in these developments to the profit not only of ourselves, but of our European friends also. But we have another role which we cannot abdicate: that of leader of the British Commonwealth. In my conception of a unified Europe, I never contemplated the diminution of the Commonwealth.

This application for membership is the sole way in which, so to speak, a reconnaissance can be carried out to find out for certain whether terms for British membership of the Community could be agreed which would meet our special needs as well as those of the Commonwealth and of our partners in the European Free Trade Area.

To sum up my views, I would say this: I think that the Government are right to apply to join the EEC, not because I am yet convinced that we shall be able to join, but because there appears to be no other way by which we can find out exactly whether the conditions of membership are acceptable.

It would not be unfair to call this a fence-sitting speech. The great man simply could not make up his mind.

In 1963, however, after de Gaulle's veto, Churchill drafted a letter to the Belgian statesman Paul-Henri Spaak, saying, 'The future of Europe if Britain were to be excluded is bleak indeed.' But he did not send the letter.[21]

It is fascinating to speculate on what Churchill's attitude would have been had he come to realize that the Commonwealth, whatever its value, could not be a substitute for Empire. The Commonwealth was not and could never be a power grouping that would give Britain superpower status comparable to that of the United States or the Soviet Union. One of Churchill's colleagues in his peacetime government, Edward Heath—later the prime minister who led Britain's successful application to join the European Community in 1973—argued in 1996 that Churchill's reluctance to join the Coal and Steel Community was 'based on circumstance; it was not opposition based on principle.'[22] And the circumstances, Heath argued, had changed. Had Churchill appreciated that Britain would not remain an imperial or a world power, he would, like de Gaulle in France, have perceived that his country's future lay with Europe. For Churchill wanted Britain to remain a power in the world. He thought it was little use being wise and benevolent if no one listened to you and you were not in a position to enforce your will.

I tend to agree with Edward Heath's view. I believe that Churchill would have come to favour Britain's membership of the European Union. But of course we shall never know. What is clear is that, even after Britain finally joined the European Community in 1973, the country was, for much of its period of membership, an awkward partner.

This may appear odd. Britain, after all, is geographically part of Europe, though many in Britain are accustomed to speak of 'Europe' when they really mean 'the Continent.' When speaking of Brexit, the country's departure from the European Union, British ministers have taken to insisting that although Britain is leaving the European Union, it is not leaving Europe! As if Britain could somehow depart from the Continent to which it belongs. And yet the British have never been able to give a definitive answer to the fundamental question—do they share in the common destiny of which Robert Schuman spoke? To Americans, the British attitude to the Continent must appear particularly odd. Dover is just twenty-seven miles from Calais, and on a clear day one can see France from the English coast. The Channel tunnel, opened in 1994, links Britain even more closely to the Continent. No doubt Europe looks more united from America than it does to Europeans themselves. The historian A.J.P. Taylor once said, 'No doubt all the inhabitants of the world look the same when viewed from the moon. All sheep look alike to us, and probably we all look alike to sheep.'[23]

Nevertheless, Britain is different; and the reasons for British attitudes towards Europe lie deep in British history, a history quite different from that of the countries of the Continent. They lie in the nature of Britain's imperial past. Britain indeed has appeared to many during the twentieth century as a different sort of power from the countries of the Continent.

At the beginning of the twentieth century, Westminster was the Parliament not only of the United Kingdom., but also of the empire. It was then often known as the Imperial Parliament. For it was the legislature of the largest land empire the world had ever seen, an empire containing, in addition to the 38 million living in Britain, some 360 million people and covering around one-fifth of the globe, around 12 million square miles out of a habitable world total of 60 million square miles. The 400 million subjects of the British Empire made up a quarter of the world's population—a larger share than either Russia or the United States. The empire had, moreover, the peculiarity that, by contrast with Rome and the compact empires of Russia and Germany, it was not land-based, created through expansion from the homeland, but a maritime empire, distributed along the world's maritime highways. Indeed, being an island, Britain had perforce to expand over ocean, in contrast to the land empires of the Continent. This meant that Britain, by contrast with the Continental powers, was a global and maritime power, not a European land power.

To the fundamental question of whether Britain is part of Europe, the answer in terms of geography must of course be 'Yes'—but what is the political answer? For much of British history it was 'No.' Going back in time to, say, 1900, almost everyone would have said that Britain was not politically part of Europe—and many felt that the less it had to do with the Continent, the better. Britain was an imperial power, and as such looked not to the Continent but to the wider world. The Continent paradoxically appeared more distant than the far-flung empire. In 1938, when it seemed that Britain might have to go to war because of a conflict between Germany and Czechoslovakia over the fate of the German-speaking inhabitants of the Sudeten areas of Czechoslovakia, Prime Minister Neville Chamberlain said in a radio broadcast to the nation, 'How horrible, fantastic, incredible, it is that we should be digging trenches and trying on gas-masks because of a quarrel in a far-away country between people of whom we know nothing.' He has been much criticised for this statement, but one may suspect that it reflected the feelings of many, perhaps the majority of people in Britain. The next year, of course, Britain was to go to war because of another quarrel in a far-away country— Poland. But perhaps the British people would not have regarded Canada, Australia, India, or South Africa, countries far more distant geographically than Czechoslovakia or Poland, but home to many of their relatives, as far-away countries. 'In every respect except distance,' Labour's National Executive declared in 1950, 'we in Britain are closer to our kinsmen in Australia and New Zealand on the far side of the world, than we are in Europe. We are closer in language, and in origins, in social habits and institutions, in political outlook and in economic interest.'[24] That is probably still true. And in 1952, Foreign

Secretary Anthony Eden, faced with pressure from the United States to join with Continental powers to build a united Europe, told his private secretary, 'What you've got to remember is that if you looked at the postbag of any English village and examined the letters coming in from abroad to the whole population, ninety per cent of them would come from way beyond Europe.'[25]

And because of Britain's island situation, its trading pattern was quite different from that of the Continental powers. As the first industrial nation, Britain had a much smaller agricultural sector than its Continental competitors. As a maritime power, the British relied on cheap food from the colonies. Their commercial system was based on free trade, unlike the high-tariff countries of the Continent, with their large agricultural sectors. Being a maritime power and an island, Britain could rely on its navy for defence. Unlike Continental countries, there was no need for a large army, so there was no conscription in peacetime until April 1939, just five months before the outbreak of the Second World War. In 1900, Britain had no troops on the Continent at all. Indeed the British did not agree to maintain troops on the Continent in time of peace until 1954. And Britain had no European alliances except with Portugal. The British lived in splendid isolation, protected by the navy and the empire. Britain was, in the words of John of Gaunt in Shakespeare's *Richard II*,

> This fortress built by Nature for herself
> Against infection and the hand of war.

The infection, presumably, came from the Continent!

The British stance towards Europe therefore remained, as Disraeli had declared it in 1872, a policy of 'reserve, but proud reserve.'[26]

Perhaps that period of isolation, though it has long gone, still retains some of its impact upon the British psyche. Perhaps

British attitudes to Europe remain 'reserve, but proud reserve,' as described by Disraeli. That at least was what President de Gaulle thought when, in January 1963, he vetoed Britain's first attempt to enter the European Communities. Sometimes perhaps one's adversaries see one's situation much more clearly than one's friends. In the press conference at which he announced his veto, de Gaulle said that the Treaty of Rome, which established the European Communities, had been signed in 1957 by six 'continental states' 'which were of the same nature.' Britain, by contrast, was 'insular, she is maritime, she is linked through her exchanges, her markets, her supply lines, to the most diverse and often the most distant countries; she pursues essentially industrial and commercial activities, and only slight agricultural ones.' That was why Britain was so opposed to the Common Agricultural Policy, which the French regarded as an essential element of the European Community. De Gaulle concluded that 'the nature, the structure, the very situation (*conjuncture*) that are England's differ profoundly from those of the continentals.' He did, admittedly, accept that Britain might evolve 'little by little towards the Continent.' And he concluded by saying that, if that happened, no one would be more pleased than France. That perhaps was not wholly sincere.

If Britain was not, in President de Gaulle's view, European, could it nevertheless become European? De Gaulle's successor as president of France, Georges Pompidou, certainly thought that it was possible. In 1971, when Prime Minister Edward Heath was making his successful attempt to secure British entry into the European Community, Pompidou declared in a television interview that he had asked Heath whether Britain had really decided to become European, whether 'Britain, which is an island, had decided to moor herself to the continent and if she was therefore ready to come in from the wide seas which had always drawn her.' And he said that Heath's response had convinced him that his views were in line with France's own conception of Europe.[27]

But did Heath's concept of the future of Europe match that held by the British people? Many would argue that it did not. They would say that France's concept of Europe, which involved a Common Agricultural Policy and a Common Fisheries Policy, fitted in well with the French conception of the future of Europe, but not with Britain's; that it would instead be in Britain's interest to have free trade in agriculture so that it could continue to import cheap food from the Commonwealth, and protection for its inefficient manufacturing industry. But the European Communities provided for the opposite—free trade in manufactures and protection in agriculture. Many would argue, therefore, that the European enterprise was not in Britain's interests at all. Moreover, while many on the Continent defined themselves as European, the British did not. The original six member states of the European Communities believed that they had more in common with each other than with outside powers. That had been the foundation for the sharing of national sovereignty. But the British tended to define themselves by contrast with Europe. So, when they finally decided to seek membership of the European Communities, they did so not because they shared in a common destiny but because they sought specific advantages. They joined on the basis of a cost-benefit analysis. But sometimes they sought the benefits without being willing to bear the accompanying costs and obligations.

Still, the twentieth century had shown that Britain could not isolate itself from the Continent. For of course the nation had fought two world wars in the twentieth century because of what happened not in the Empire, but in Europe—in those far-away countries of which we knew nothing. On both occasions, Britain fought in alliance with France, in large part to preserve the independence of France and also of Belgium, whose neutrality was violated by Germany in 1914. Britain did so because its government and people took the view that their independence would be worth little if a hostile power were to control France, the Channel ports, or the Low Countries. By that reasoning, surely Britain's future depended not on what happened in Canada, Australia, India, or Africa but on what happened on the Continent.

Nevertheless, the main events which have stamped British consciousness are events that occurred when Britain was alone confronting a hostile Continent—during the Napoleonic wars and of course in 1940, when British troops were successfully evacuated from the Continent at Dunkirk. It is a measure perhaps of Britain's reluctance to involve itself in the Continent that the evacuation at Dunkirk was so widely seen not as a defeat but as a triumph, as some sort of victory. After the fall of France, which put Britain in mortal danger of invasion, George VI wrote to his mother, 'Personally I feel happier now that we have no allies to be polite to and pamper.' And, adds the king's official biographer, 'in these sentiments [he] was at one with the vast majority of his subjects.'

The events of 1940 seemed to show that Britain did not stand or fall as a nation with the other nations of the Continent. Unlike them, the country could survive a military defeat because of the English Channel. Britain could withdraw its troops from Europe and, unlike the countries of the Continent, remain in the war. Because it was an island, Britain was free to carry on the fight. Perhaps it was less similar to the Continental states than to Russia. For Russia also, as the wars against Napoleon and Hitler showed, could survive military defeat because of its huge immensity as part of the vast Eurasian land mass.

The outcome of the Second World War further emphasised the contrasts between Britain and the Continent. Alone amongst the European powers except for Russia—a part-European power—Britain was a victor in the war. Furthermore, Britain was the only one of the European combatants which had neither been ruled by a Fascist or Nazi government nor been invaded and occupied by the Nazi or Fascist powers. In consequence, it was the only one of the European powers whose institutions had remained intact through the war. The other countries had to start again. They had to adopt new constitutions; they also had to come to terms with the experience of Fascism, Nazism, or collaboration. To put the point somewhat crudely, young people on the Continent had to ask themselves whether they could be proud of what their parents or grandparents had done during the war, or whether shame was a more appropriate reaction. 'Being European,' the Bulgarian political scientist Ivan Krastev has said, 'is about being aware of what we did.'[28] Europeans needed to overcome the past by creating new institutions, not only in their own countries but across Europe, new transnational institutions to ensure that the future of the continent would be brighter than the past. The sense of being European was 'a state of mind born of defeat, occupation and the gulf between those who collaborated and those who resisted.'[29]

Britain did not share this state of mind. Through the accident of geography, the British could be proud, not ashamed of their part in the war. And indeed, in the early postwar years, Britain saw itself, together with the United States and the Soviet Union, as one of the three great powers in the world. Had its leaders not taken part in the great wartime conferences at Tehran, Yalta, and Potsdam—conferences at which Europe had not been represented? 'What is noteworthy,' a former ambassador to the United States declared in the mid-1950s, 'is the way that we take this [Britain's great-power status] for granted. It is not a belief arrived at after reflection by a conscious decision. It is part of the habit and furniture of our minds; a principle so much at one with our outlook and character that it determines the way we act without emerging itself into clear consciousness.'[30] But that status was not taken for granted abroad, where the facts of the loss of empire and Britain's economic weakness were becoming painfully apparent.

So there was a huge difference in national psychology between Britain and the countries of the Continent. Further, while Europe was profoundly aware of its weakness, Britain was full of optimism and self-confidence, both of which were gradually to decline during the postwar years. Tony Benn, a left-wing Labour MP, called the volume of his diaries dealing with the 1950s *Years of Hope*. I once asked him why, given that the Labour Party was in opposition for most of the 1950s, he had given his book that title. He replied that one should remember the huge scale of British achievements during the immediate postwar years. Not only had Britain won the war, it had also secured full employment after it and created a National Health Service and a welfare state. The nation had ensured collective security through the NATO alliance and by supporting the United States in Korea. There seemed at that time almost nothing that Britain could not achieve.

That confidence began to fade after the failed Suez expedition in 1956, and was then to fall further under the impact of economic difficulties. But the psychology of self-confidence was well expressed by Clement Attlee, prime minister in the postwar Labour government, in his last public speech in 1967, shortly before his death. He had been asked to speak to the Labour Party's Common Market Safeguards Committee, a euphemistic title for a body which was opposed to Britain joining the European Community. His speech was typically short and laconic. He said: 'The Common Market. The so-called Common Market of six nations. Know them all well. Very recently this country spent a great deal of blood and treasure rescuing four of 'em from the other two.'[31] And then he sat down!

The point may be put in another way by a critic of British policy, Jean Monnet, who always regretted that Britain had not played a more positive role in Europe. 'Britain,' he said, 'had not been conquered or invaded. She felt no need to exorcise history.'[32] The Second World War helped to instil into the British consciousness the idea that its commitment to the Continent was bound to be limited, that it could never be a total commitment. From this point of view, perhaps de Gaulle was right after all, and Pompidou was wrong in the belief that Edward Heath—or indeed anyone else—could make Britain view itself as a wholly European power.

It was not that Britain was an uncooperative partner in Europe. Quite the contrary. After 1945, Britain was to play a leading role in the reconstruction of Europe and in helping to create an alliance system based on collective security. Whereas the government had refused, before both world wars, to join a formal alliance with France, in 1948 Britain signed the Treaty of Brussels, a treaty of alliance with France and the Benelux countries. This was expanded in 1949 into the NATO alliance, which involved a unified command and an explicit commitment to collective security, so that an attack on any of the members of the alliance, which included most of the western European powers, was to be regarded as an attack on all; and its members were under an obligation to go to the aid of any country that was attacked. This again was a great contrast to policy in the period before the two world wars, when Britain was adamant in not accepting a Continental commitment. And, in 1949, Britain played a leading part in the establishment of a new intergovernmental institution, the Council of Europe, and in framing the European Convention on Human Rights. But none of these commitments involved the sharing of power or supra-nationalism. None of them involved a transfer of parliamentary sovereignty. Indeed, the Council of Europe was to be distinguished from the European Communities precisely because it did *not* involve such a transfer. 'We are willing,' declared Clement Attlee, 'to play an active part in all forms of European cooperation on an intergovernmental basis but cannot surrender our freedom of decision and action to any supranational authority.'[33]

Britain continued to see itself as a global and not a wholly European power. Winston Churchill, in opposition after 1945, told the Conservative Party Conference in 1948 that Britain's strength derived from being at the centre of three circles of influence. 'As I look upon the future of our country in the changing scene of human destiny I feel the existence of three great circles among the free nations and democracies. The first circle for us is naturally the British Commonwealth and Empire, with all that that comprises. Then there is also the English-speaking world in which we, Canada, and the other British Dominions play so important a part. And finally, there is United Europe. These three majestic circles are co-existent and if they are linked together there is no force or combination which could overthrow them or ever challenge them. Now if you think of the three interlinked circles you will see that we are the only country which has a great part in every one of them. We stand, in fact, at the very point of junction and here in this island at the centre of the seaways, and perhaps of the airways also we have the opportunity of joining them all together.'[34]

The key to British power and influence, Churchill believed—and his belief was shared by most of the Conservative Party—was to hold these three relationships in balance, to remain at the centre of all three circles and not cut loose from any of them. Any tilt in the direction of one of these relationships would put the other relationships at risk, and so weaken British power. In particular, a merging of sovereignty with the Continental powers would compromise, it was thought, the United Kingdom's position as head of the Commonwealth. As

a Foreign Office official told a Labour minister in 1950 in relation to the Schuman plan, 'We shall have tipped the balance
against the other two elements in our world-situation, the Atlantic Community and the Commonwealth. It is not for nothing that M. Schuman's original memorandum said in terms and
repeatedly that his plan would be a step towards the federation
of Europe.'[35] So Britain, although it could be a good alliance
partner with the Continent, could not merge its sovereignty
with other European powers. Britain could not commit itself
to a specifically European orientation.

As a great power, Churchill believed, Britain could maintain a 'special relationship' with the United States. That was
something that Churchill, with his American mother, was bound
to feel with particular intensity. Indeed, Churchill was sometimes described as half American and all British! Interestingly,
one of his successors as prime minister, Harold Macmillan, also
had an American mother. In the nineteenth century, Bismarck
had said that the key to the twentieth century would be that the
Americans spoke English. The years of Churchill's active political life—from 1900 to 1955—were also the years when, in
British eyes at least, the special relationship was at its closest.
Churchill believed, with some reason, that a strong alliance
between Britain and the United States could have prevented
both world wars, just as, in the postwar world, it was proving
instrumental in preventing a third world war with the Soviet
Union. But Churchill went even further than this. He hoped for
some sort of political union, ill-defined admittedly, between the
Commonwealth and the United States: a union of the English-
speaking peoples. In 1958, he concluded the fourth and final
volume of *A History of the English-Speaking Peoples* with the
words: 'The future is unknowable, but the past should give us
hope. Nor should we seek to define precisely *the exact terms of
ultimate union*' (emphasis added).[36]

Of course, Britain alone could not hope to match the power and wealth of the United States, but as Churchill had said in a speech in November 1949, 'Britain cannot be thought of as a single state in isolation. She is the founder and centre of a world-wide Empire and Commonwealth.' But the Commonwealth could never be a power bloc as the Empire seemed to have been. It could constrain British policy, but it could hardly strengthen it. Britain was no longer an imperial power. This meant that Britain could no longer remain a global power. That, however, was a conclusion Churchill was unwilling to accept. Union with the United States was of course quite unrealistic, and the Americans never took it seriously. In early 1953, after Churchill's visit to the United States for talks with Dwight D. Eisenhower, his wartime comrade, the president-elect wrote in his diary that Churchill had 'developed an almost childlike faith that all of the answers are to be found merely in British-American partnership,' and that 'Winston is trying to relive the days of World War II.'[37] In 1954, after speaking with Churchill, Secretary of State John Foster Dulles told Eisenhower: 'The Prime Minister followed his usual line. He said only the English-speaking peoples counted, that together they could rule the world.'[38] Postwar American governments, whether Republican or Democrat, believed that it would be best for Britain to cease trying to play an independent power role, and join the movement for European integration so as to strengthen the Western European arm of the Atlantic alliance. Indeed, both the Eisenhower and Kennedy administrations tried to push British governments in this direction. The Suez crisis of October 1956, just eighteen months after Churchill's retirement as prime minister, showed that the special relationship with the United States, if it existed at all, was one between superior and subordinate; and it demolished the idea that Britain remained a great power. For Britain found that it could not, in conjunction with

France, carry out a military expedition opposed by the United States. The relationship, therefore, could never be one between equals.

Churchill understood that the war had undermined Britain's international position. But he saw it as a temporary phenomenon, something that could be transformed through an act of will, just as he had transformed Britain's desperate situation in 1940 through an act of will. He did not accept that the war had permanently undermined the country's international position, so that Britain would not remain a great power in its aftermath. The British could never return to their prewar role, and indeed many of their problems arose from trying to do so. Churchill could not fully appreciate that the era of empire, even though it had so strongly coloured Britain's sense of national identity for so many years, was an aberrant period in the country's long history. Britain's imperial experience, importance as it was, was nevertheless a deviation, while its link to the Continent was a fundamental axiom of its existence.

Churchill saw as one of the central purposes of his political career, as he put it in 1940, 'the maintenance of the enduring greatness of Britain and her Empire.'[39] Yet the central theme of his entire political career, all the way up to 1955, was the *decline* of British power. Perhaps this decline was inevitable— perhaps no one could have arrested it—but it was decline all the same. And Churchill recognised it. He told a political colleague, Lord Boothby, towards the end of his life: 'Historians are apt to judge war ministers less by the victories achieved under their direction than by the political results which flowed from them. Judged by that standard, I am not sure that I shall be held to have done very well.'[40]

In retirement, he told his private secretary, Anthony Montague Browne, that he was a failure. When Browne demurred, perhaps thinking that the old man was gaga, Churchill said, 'I have worked very hard all my life, and I have achieved a great deal—in the end to achieve NOTHING'—the last word, according to Browne, 'falling with sombre emphasis.'[41] And in 1979, just fourteen years after Churchill's death, the retiring British ambassador in Paris, Sir Nicholas Henderson, was to write sadly in his valedictory despatch, 'Our decline in relation to our European partners has been so marked that today we are not only no longer a world power, but we are not in the first rank even as a European one.'[42]

The Labour Party did not disagree in principle with Churchill's view. In the late 1940s, the empire was in the process of being transformed by Clement Attlee's Labour government into a multiracial Commonwealth, symbolised by the independence of India in 1947 and its entry in 1949 into the Commonwealth as a republic—the first republic to be admitted. The Labour Party had an emotional involvement with India, whose independence it had long supported, but also with the older dominions such as Canada and Australia, based on their support in two world wars. Attlee's successor as Labour leader, Hugh Gaitskell, declared in a speech to the Labour Party conference in 1962, at a time when the Conservative government was seeking to take Britain into the European Communities, 'We at least shall not forget Gallipoli and Vimy Ridge.' What he meant was that if a European orientation involved sacrificing Commonwealth interests, it should be rejected.

The psychological and sentimental attachment to the Commonwealth was reinforced in the early postwar period by a system of Imperial Preference, which enabled goods from Commonwealth countries to enter Britain either duty free or at lower tariff rates than goods from third countries. Such a system was clearly incompatible with the European Economic Community, which was a customs union and demanded a uniform tariff from all its members against third countries. But the Commonwealth's importance to Britain was by no means solely geopolitical or economic. It was and is also emotional and sentimental, based on ties of family and friendship. There are today more British people living in Australia alone than in the other twenty-seven European Union countries combined. Opinion poll after opinion poll has shown that the countries to which the British feel closest are not those of the Continent, but Canada, Australia, and New Zealand. So, although Britain trades far more with the European Union than it does with Canada, Australia, or New Zealand, the ties of sentiment are stronger and more profound than the ties linking Britain with the Continent.[43]

In 1949, Robert Schuman had said that without Britain there can be no Europe. But the success of the Coal and Steel Community showed that without Britain there *could* be a Europe. If the British did not want to join, so be it. Others would move ahead without them. Monnet had told the British chancellor of the Exchequer, Sir Stafford Cripps, in May 1950: 'I hope with all my heart that you will join in this from the start. But, if you don't we shall go ahead without you. And I'm sure that because you are realists, you will adjust to the facts when you see that we have succeeded.'[44] But if Britain later decided to participate, it would have to accept rules drawn up by others. France and Germany would be the motors of European cooperation. They, not Britain, would be the dominant powers in the new Europe. Britain would be outside, and although it would eventually seek to join, it would do so as a supplicant, a country seeking favours.

In 1956, the Suez crisis led to a further divergence between British and French attitudes. For Britain, the failure of the Suez expedition brought the lesson that the nation needed to regenerate what it still thought of as a special relationship with the United States. But the French drew a different lesson. Konrad

Adenauer, chancellor of Germany, told French foreign minister Christian Pineau on 6 November 1956, just after the failure had become clear, that for Britain, France, and Germany, there was 'only one way of playing a decisive role in the world. That is to unite Europe. . . . We have no time to waste. Make Europe your revenge.'[45] The French took Adenauer's advice. For the French, the founders of Europe included not only Jean Monnet and Joseph Stalin (whose threats had provided a powerful incentive for European unity) but also President Nasser of Egypt. Indeed, as the historian Quinn Slobodian writes, 'a French observer quipped that a statue should be raised to Egyptian leader Gamal Abdel Nasser as the federator of Europe; for nationalising the canal and creating the conditions for the largest Western European powers to bond.'[46] So while Britain, under the new prime minister Harold Macmillan, made haste to repair relations with the United States so that it could become, in Macmillan's somewhat patronizing comment, the Greece to their Rome, France devoted its energies to constructing a dominating position in Europe. The British did not seem to understand their changed geopolitical position. Britain, Adenauer caustically remarked in 1956, had become like 'a rich man who has lost all his property but does not realise it.'[47]

Two divergent conclusions are possible. The first is that it was foolish for Britain to have lost the leadership of Europe. American secretary of state Dean Acheson called it 'the greatest mistake of the post-war period.'[48] The second conclusion is that it was the right decision—since, if Britain had joined, it would have faced similar problems to those that it actually did face when it joined the European Community in 1973. The Eurosceptics would argue that the European commitment, not the refusal, was Britain's basic mistake. But this view has to confront the fact that since the premiership of Harold Macmillan in 1961, every single British prime minister until Boris Johnson in 2019 has thought that it would be best for Britain to be part of the European Communities or the European Union.

Nevertheless, when the Treaty of Rome established the European Communities in 1957, only the small Liberal Party, with just 6 seats out of 630 in the House of Commons, suggested that Britain should join. Those who would later advocate membership were at that time adamantly opposed. In November 1956, for example, Harold Macmillan, then chancellor of the Exchequer, told the Commons: 'I do not believe that this House would ever agree to our entering arrangements which, as a matter of principle, would prevent our treating the great range of imports from the Commonwealth at least as favourably as those from the European countries. So this objection, even if there were no other, would be quite fatal to any proposal that the United Kingdom should seek to take part in a European Common Market by joining a Customs Union. . . . So that is out.'[49] Reginald Maudling, president of the Board of Trade, told the Commons in February 1959: 'We must recognise that for us to sign the Treaty of Rome would be to accept as the ultimate goal political federation in Europe, including ourselves. That . . . does not seem to me to be a proposition which, at the moment, commands majority support in this country.'[50] In the 1959 general election, the first after the establishment of the European Communities, none of the party manifestoes suggested that Britain should join—not even that of the Liberal Party, which was to become the most enthusiastically pro-European of all the British parties. Its election manifesto said nothing at all about Europe.

Had Britain been in a position to sign the Treaty of Rome, it would have faced considerable problems, since its political and economic structures were so different from those of the other six countries. Nevertheless, it would have joined before the Common Agricultural Policy and the formula for financial contributions were agreed. When it finally did join, Britain had to accept conditions of membership that were not necessarily in its interest. Being present at the creation would almost certainly have ensured less disadvantageous conditions. Geopolitically, the Britain of 1958 would have been in a strong position to counter the hegemony of a France still entangled in Algeria and about to face a transition from the Fourth to the Fifth Republic. And perhaps the institutions of Europe would have reflected British traditions more than French. Britain would have been able to help to shape a European future for itself. But the issue received very little public discussion. By contrast with the long and somewhat tortured discussion in government of the Schuman Plan in Britain, it was taken for granted in 1958 that Britain should not join the European Communities. The decision not to join was a mere reaffirmation of existing policy. To have joined would have involved a radical discontinuity of approach, an imaginative leap, perhaps a leap of faith. For a commitment to the Continent did not follow from Britain's traditional understanding of its international position.

In 1955, a former British ambassador to the United States wrote: 'We thought that the old Europe of independent quarrelling sovereign nations was continuing. It was not. Something novel was happening, and perhaps British leaders were at fault in not recognising it.'[51] Europe was congealing into a new shape. Britain was never wholly comfortable with this new shape. The British were to remain good Europeans in the sense of being *in* Europe and being committed to European security. But they never became good Europeans in the sense of being *of* Europe. The British attitude towards European integration did not fundamentally alter during more than forty-six years of membership of the European Community and European Union. Britain was always uncertain—half in, half out, generally opposed to further integration, but unable to suggest an alternative which commanded real enthusiasm on the Continent. The pattern was set, for better or worse, in the 1950s. Moves on the Continent towards European unity were seen as a problem rather than as a challenge, much less an inspiration.

2

The Pandora's Box and the Trojan Horses
Britain in Europe

The foreign secretary in Britain's postwar Labour government was Ernest Bevin, a former trade union leader and a man noted for his colourful turn of phrase. When, in 1949, he was asked whether Britain should join the Council of Europe, which he mistakenly thought would be a supranational body, he told his officials, 'I don't like it.' He explained why: 'If you open that Pandora's box, you never know what Trojan 'orses will fly out.'[1] The British government helped to ensure that the Council of Europe was an innocuous and purely advisory body. To that, Bevin had no objection. But his remark was perhaps the most prescient ever made about Britain's involvement with the movement for European integration.

Europe has proved a poisoned chalice for British governments since Harold Macmillan first sought to enter the European Communities in 1961. He had hoped that entry would prove a good election cry for a modernising government against the Labour opposition, which at that time was Eurosceptic. But de Gaulle's veto of the British application in 1963 helped to destroy Macmillan's government. De Gaulle correctly predicted that Labour would win the next election. His information minister, Alain Peyrefitte, records him saying: 'That Macmillan vanishes!' He then sliced the air with the back of his hand, 'as pitiless as a Roman emperor turning down his thumb as though denying a reprieve to a defeated gladiator.'[2]

Edward Heath was the Conservative prime minister who took Britain into the European Communities in 1973, following de Gaulle's second veto in 1967. But in February 1974, Heath was narrowly defeated in a general election. In the case of a narrow defeat, any of a number of factors might be responsible, but one of them was almost certainly opposition to his policy on Europe, which many associated with rising food prices. The opposition Labour Party was calling for a referendum on Britain's membership, and this was supported by a former Conservative minister, Enoch Powell, who had won much popularity, particularly with working-class voters, for his attack on high levels of Commonwealth immigration. Powell had opposed British entry and, in the general election of February 1974, he recommended a vote for Labour so that there would be a chance of taking Britain out of the European Community in a referendum. Europe, therefore, was undoubtedly one cause of Heath's fall.

Margaret Thatcher, Heath's successor as Conservative leader, became prime minister in 1979 and gradually turned into a Eurosceptic. In November 1990 this fact was to lead to the resignation from her Cabinet of her deputy, Sir Geoffrey Howe. That resignation provoked a leadership challenge, which led to Margaret Thatcher's own resignation. Her successor, John Major, declared that he wanted Britain to be at the heart of Europe, but his government was riven in two by divisions over ratification of the Maastricht treaty of 1992 and the divisive issue of European monetary cooperation. These divisions were a major cause of the Conservatives' landslide defeat in 1997. Europe, one former Conservative minister declared, was becoming 'a Bermuda triangle for the Conservative Party.'[3] The next Conservative prime minister, David Cameron, who came to power in 2010, proposed, in 2013, a referendum that would resolve the European issue once and for all. But that referendum, in 2016, resulted in a 52 percent to 48 percent vote to leave the European Union. Cameron immediately resigned. His successor, Theresa May, found Brexit to be the all-consuming theme of her government. She too had to cope with divisions in her Cabinet and her party, reflecting a country that remains deeply divided over Europe. She too was compelled to drink from the poisoned chalice. She too was forced to resign, in 2019, because of her failure to resolve the issue.

Europe, therefore, has been responsible for ruining the premiership of six of the last seven Conservative leaders of Great Britain: Macmillan, Heath, Thatcher, Major, Cameron, and May. The only Conservative prime minister since 1961 not to be so undone was Sir Alec Douglas-Home, and he served for just one year between 1963 and 1964.

Nor has the Labour Party proved immune to the European virus. During the 1970s, indeed, it appeared that Labour was even more divided on Europe than the Conservatives. The left wing of the party was hostile to the European Community and pressed the party's leader, Harold Wilson, to concede a referendum in 1975 on whether Britain should remain. After Labour's defeat in the general election of 1979, the left wing gained influence, and in the 1983 general election, which Labour lost, the party committed itself to leaving the European Community without a referendum. This trend towards Euroscepticism was one of the factors that had caused, in 1981, a breakaway from Labour by some of the leaders of the pro-European faction, including former senior ministers Roy Jenkins, Shirley Williams, and David Owen. They formed a new party, the Social Democratic Party, fighting elections in alliance with the pro-European Liberals and eventually merging with them in 1988 to form the Liberal Democrats. After 2015, Labour was also divided, although, being in opposition, its divisions were more hidden. Indeed, in 2019, believing that Jeremy Corbyn, the Labour leader, was insufficiently committed to the Remain cause, a small group of Labour MPs left the party and joined some Conservative defectors to form a new party, Change UK, to campaign for a second referendum that might overturn the results of the first. But all lost their seats in the general election of 2019.

Europe, then, has proved toxic for both of Britain's major political parties, and for British governments of both right and left. It has added the poison of intra-party conflict to the normal adversarial politics between the parties. Further, one suspects, its possibility for disruption has not yet been exhausted. Brexit, after all, is a process, not an event, and it is a process that is likely to continue for some years. It is an issue like Home Rule at the end of the nineteenth century and tariff reform at the beginning of the twentieth: capable of realigning politics, splitting parties, and destroying political careers.

Europe is as toxic as these older issues for the very simple reason that all of them raise fundamental questions of identity and sovereignty. They strike at the very roots of the British conception of themselves. Europe forces Britons to ask, Is being British compatible with being European?

The European Communities, or Common Market—precursor of the European Union—came into existence in 1958, following the Treaty of Rome signed in 1957. There were originally just six members—France, Germany, Italy, and the Benelux countries—the same countries that had joined the European Coal and Steel Community. Britain did not join in 1958. But in 1961, Prime Minister Harold Macmillan decided to make an application to join, a decision characterised by the former prime minister, Anthony Eden, now Lord Avon, as economically 'more important than any decision since the repeal of the Corn Laws [in 1846]. On the political side, it can be more important than any decision we have taken in our history.'[4]

The British, then, found themselves unable to ignore this important new development, which was, as it were, on their doorstep. What should their attitude be? Britain had not joined the Coal and Steel Community but had wished it well. It was after all in Britain's interest if this new development helped ensure peace on the Continent. Moreover, the strengthening of Western Europe would help in its defence, and enable it better to meet the Soviet threat. Indeed, the need to strengthen and integrate Western Europe was one of the reasons postwar American administrations, whether Democratic or Republican, pressed for European unity. The Marshall Plan had been premised on the idea that the Western European states would come together to organise their economies. The American administrator of the plan said that its aim was to get Europe 'on its feet and off our backs.'[5] And George C. Marshall himself claimed to have been influenced by Churchill's Zurich speech on a united Europe when he made his call for aid to the continent.[6]

British opinion on the early stages of European development was perhaps best summed up by the diplomat who wrote that it would be 'wrong in the present state of morale in Europe, for Her Majesty's Government to take up a position which obstructs the endeavours of other European Powers to achieve closer unity. . . . Traditionally, British policy has always been to prevent the formation of any such grouping in the Continent, but the emergence of the Soviet Union as an overriding threat to Europe has altered the basis on which this policy was founded.'[7] This marked a fundamental change in British foreign policy. Previously, Britain had supported a balance of power on the Continent in which no single power or bloc should be allowed to dominate. But Europe now faced a different problem: to ensure that a strong European voice would be heard in a world dominated by the two superpowers. The problem seemed no longer one of preventing the emergence of a predominant power on the Continent, but of ensuring that Europe had a voice in the world and that Britain's voice would also be heard.

Gradually, however, it came to be appreciated that if Britain remained aloof, the European economic union would pose a threat both to the power of Britain in the world and to the British economy. In his memoirs, describing European efforts towards integration in the early 1950s, Harold Macmillan wrote:

> I frankly hoped and believed that they would break down. If they were successful, it might be a short-term advantage, especially if it facilitated immediate German rearmament. But the long-term future would be grim indeed. There would be a European Community, from which we should be excluded, and which would effectively control Europe. This was the historic struggle in which we had been engaged first against Louis XIV, then against Napoleon, and twice in our lifetime against Germany. Germany was weak now; in the long run she would be stronger than France; and so we might be bringing about in twenty years' time that domination of Europe by Germany to prevent which we had made such terrible sacrifices twice within a single generation. It should therefore be our hope that the Schuman Plan . . . would fail.[8]

In March 1953, Macmillan asked the Cabinet, 'Are we really sure that we want to see a six-Power Federal Europe, with a common army, a common iron and steel industry (Schuman Plan) . . . ending in a common currency and monetary policy? If such a Federal State comes into being, will it, in the long run, be to our interest, whether as an island or as an imperial Power? Will not Germany ultimately control this state, and may we not have created the very situation in Europe to prevent which, in every century, since the Elizabethan age, we have fought long and bitter wars?'[9] It was not, on this view, in Britain's interests that the process of European integration should succeed; but if it did succeed, then perhaps Britain might have no alternative but to join it, based on the old aphorism, if you can't beat them, join them. That was the dilemma Macmillan was to face during his premiership, which began in 1957.

Macmillan's first reaction to the formation of the European Communities was to try to dilute it, to transform it into something intergovernmental. In 1958 he proposed, in place of the European Communities, a Free Trade Area, a plan for free trade in industrial goods among all of the seventeen free powers of western Europe. Agriculture would not be included. There would be no Common Agricultural Policy and no common external tariff. So the free trade area would not affect British imports of cheap food from the Commonwealth. In addition, there would be no political implications. The preamble to the Treaty of Rome spoke of the six member states of the Common Market proceeding to 'ever closer union.' There would be nothing like that in the Free Trade Area.

But, for these very reasons, the Free Trade Area idea did not appeal to the Six. For, with free trade in manufactures, but not in agriculture, it would mean that British goods could enter the industrial markets of the Continent tariff-free, while the produce of Continental farmers would not enter the British market tariff-free. The opposition to the Free Trade Area was led by France, even before de Gaulle came to power in 1958.

But French hostility became even stronger in the Fifth Republic, established by de Gaulle in 1958; and it was de Gaulle who put an end to negotiations for the Free Trade Area. De Gaulle later wrote in his memoir that Macmillan 'declared to me with great feeling: "The Common Market is the Continental System all over again. Britain cannot accept it. I beg you to give it up. Otherwise we shall be embarking on a war, which will doubtless be economic at first but which runs the risk of gradually spreading into other fields!" '[10] Threats of this kind were unlikely to make any impact upon the French president.

But Macmillan's threat was a clear sign that Britain was losing its position of leadership in Europe. Britain was no longer, as with the discussions on the Coal and Steel Community, being asked to assume leadership in Europe. The leadership now seemed to be with France, and Britain was seeking favours which were not being granted. Britain had become a supplicant, a power on the outside looking in—as it has been, once again, in the Brexit process.

After the failure of the Free Trade Area negotiations, Britain took the lead in creating a free trade area with six other countries not in the Common Market: Denmark, Norway, Sweden, Austria, Portugal, and Switzerland. These formed the European Free Trade Association. The EFTA had free trade in industrial but not agricultural goods, no common external tariff, and no pretensions to political unity. It was perhaps a second best. Europe was now divided between two organisations—the European Communities of the Six, and the European Free Trade Association of the Seven. It did not take long for people to say that Europe was now at sixes and sevens. But the seven were in a weak, peripheral position, while the six comprised a strong centre, since it contained the major west European powers with the exception of Britain, which was outside a major new power grouping, and seemed to be on the periphery of Europe. For the first time since the Napoleonic era, the major continental powers seemed to be united in a positive economic grouping which, while not specifically directed against Britain, could exclude it both from European markets and from consultation on European policy. In July 1960, Macmillan began to confide, in the privacy of his diary, that Britain might have to join the European Communities. 'Shall we be caught between a hostile (or at least less and less friendly) America,' he wrote, 'and a boastful powerful "Empire of Charlemagne"—now under French and later bound to come under German control? Is this the real reason for "joining" the Common Market (if we are acceptable)? . . . It's a grim choice.'[11] Then, in 1961, just two years after the 1959 general election, in which Europe had not been an issue, Macmillan made that grim choice and decided that Britain must apply to join the European Communities. The Labour opposition effectively came out against any such entry by laying down conditions which it would be impossible to achieve. But in government six years later, in 1967, Labour too applied to join. Since then, every single prime minister until Boris Johnson has thought that Britain's future lay with Europe. No prime minister until Theresa May advocated leaving the European Union—and Theresa May did so only after being instructed by the British people in a referendum[12]

The key question, then, is why both parties and many of Britain's leading politicians altered their minds between 1959, when all agreed that Britain could have nothing to do with the European Communities, and 1970, when all three major parties in that year's general election agreed that Britain should join.

There was one great difference between 1959 and 1970— the steady loss of British self-confidence following the Suez crisis of 1956, a crisis which showed that Britain was not as powerful as many thought and that it could not carry out a major military intervention against the wishes of the United States. Britain was certainly no longer a superpower. It had lost the leadership position in world affairs which it had seemed to enjoy before the Second World War. The government now had to prevent the Six supplanting Britain as a superpower, and, as such, a principal influence on American policy.

By 1961, the Commonwealth included fourteen independent states and forty-five British dependencies. It had no common institutions and few common interests, and was far from being politically unified. Indeed, it was just as likely to oppose Britain as to offer support. At the time of Suez, the only Commonwealth members to take Britain's side were Australia and New Zealand. The new Commonwealth members in Asia and Africa, led by India, were united in vehement opposition to British policy. Nor was the Commonwealth a coherent economic unit. Some of its members had established protectionist policies of their own, and there was little chance of creating a single economic unit from the diverse member states that made up the new multiracial Commonwealth.

In 1960, Britain suffered two further blows to its prestige. First, the nation's position as an independent nuclear power was put into question when the Blue Streak missile program was cancelled. Britain would henceforth be dependent on the United States for the missiles needed for its nuclear weapons. So the policy of preserving Britain's great power status by maintaining an independent nuclear deterrent was coming to be severely qualified. Second, the summit conference between the United States and the Soviet Union, which Macmillan had striven hard to arrange and which he hoped would ameliorate the Cold War, collapsed when the Americans would not apologise for sending spy planes over Soviet territory. Macmillan had sought to conciliate the two superpowers, but his entreaties had been in vain. After President Eisenhower refused to apologise,

Nikita Khrushchev, leader of the Soviet Union, refused to reconsider his decision to abandon the summit. The failure of the summit, Macmillan told his biographer, was 'the most tragic moment of my life,' for, with its collapse, the prime minister, according to his private secretary, 'suddenly realised that Britain counted for nothing.'[13]

Britain's problems, as Americans saw them, were well summarised in a speech made by former secretary of state Dean Acheson at West Point in 1962, when he declared, 'Britain has lost an empire and not yet found a role.' He went on to say: 'The attempt to play a separate role—that is, a role apart from Europe, a role based on a "special relationship" with the United States, a role based on being the head of a "Commonwealth," which has no political structure, or unity, or strength, and enjoys a fragile and precarious economic relationship by means of the Sterling area and preferences in the British market—this role is about to be played out. Great Britain attempting to work alone and to be a broker between the United States and Russia, has seemed to conduct a policy as weak as its military power.'

This speech caused much resentment in Britain, but perhaps that was because it was articulating a painful truth.

Europe, then, was coming to seem the only geopolitical solution to Britain's strategic dilemmas.

But British self-confidence had been damaged not only by strategic problems but also as a result of economic difficulties. The 1950s had seemed an age of affluence, and the ruling Conservatives had won the general election of 1959 with an increased majority through the slogan 'Life's Better with the Conservatives—Don't Let Labour Ruin It.' But soon afterwards, doubts set in. During the early 1960s, it seemed that the six member states of the European Communities were progressing more rapidly than Britain and were enjoying a higher rate of economic growth. It seemed that new policies were needed.

There was a reappraisal of Britain's economic policy, with more state planning and an attempt to reach an agreement with the trade unions on wages policy. Entry into the European Communities seemed an important part of this reappraisal, since it was felt that the Common Market could, by opening up European markets, help rejuvenate British industry and so improve the nation's rate of economic growth. Europe, therefore, seemed to offer an answer not only to Britain's geopolitical dilemmas but also to the economic ones.

Britain was seeking to enter the Communities, however, not because it had come to a positive belief in the virtues of integration—the British were still far from accepting Schuman's view of a common destiny—but because they had run out of alternatives. They were now desperately seeking to avoid slipping down further in international position. In addition, the decision to seek membership was to impose strains on the Conservative Party. It was not a decision 'arising out of urges from the traditional streams of influence in the Conservative Party.' Instead, it 'flew in the face of most of the instincts of the Conservative Party, and of many of the traditional interests supporting it.'[14] It was a pragmatic decision. If at any time the costs appeared to outweigh the benefits there would be popular pressure to leave—as was to occur after 2010, reaching its culmination in the referendum of 2016.

When Harold Macmillan decided in 1961 that Britain's future lay with the European Communities, he encountered fundamental difficulties, difficulties which perhaps have never been fully resolved. Perhaps they never could have been resolved. The essence of the problem was one of fitting Britain into a Continental system whose assumptions about constitutions, politics, and economics were so different from those held in Britain. Perhaps the most fundamental problem was that of fitting a constitutional system based on the sovereignty of Parliament and the absence of a codified constitution into a Europe based on a written constitution, separation of powers, and subordination of the legal systems of the member states to a superior system of European law. The Italian political scientist Sergio Fabbrini has labelled the European Union a compound democracy, since it has a constitutionally defined separation of powers at the centre as well as a territorial division of powers. This system has some parallels to that of the United States. But while perhaps the prophet of the American system of division of powers is James Madison, and the European Union is also constructed on somewhat Madisonian lines, the prophet of the British system of government is Thomas Hobbes, the ideologist of a sovereignty undivided and absolute.[15] The sovereignty of Parliament lies at the heart of the British constitution and makes it difficult for the British to comprehend a division of powers among separate institutions, much less the subordination of Westminster to a superior legal order such as that of the European Communities. The conflict between the two conceptions of government sometimes seemed to recede into the background, but it never disappeared. More often, it moved to the foreground, as with the demand in Britain to restrict immigration from the European Union, something Parliament could not do as long as Britain remained a member state.[16]

There were, in addition, the interrelated problems of agriculture and the Commonwealth. The basic problem concerning agriculture was that Britain's system of agricultural protection had evolved in a quite different way from that of the Continent. Britain had a small agricultural sector, making up just 3.6 percent of the economy. In France, by contrast, agriculture was almost one-fifth of the economy, in Italy one-quarter, and in Germany one-eighth. Because of its small agricultural sector, Britain had to import around half of its domestic food requirements. Britain was much more reliant than Continental countries on imported food, much of which came from the Commonwealth, primarily from Canada, Australia, and New Zealand. Indeed, Britain in 1961 imported more food than all of the six member states of the European Communities put together. Since 1932, Britain had benefited from Imperial Preference from the Commonwealth, and the policy of cheap food had been a fundamental principle since the repeal of the Corn Laws in 1846. Cheap food had seemed, indeed, to be the basis of the country's nineteenth-century prosperity.

Agriculture was, admittedly, given economic support by the British government. That, however, was done not through tariffs but by means of subsidies to domestic agriculture, so-called deficiency payments, paid for by the taxpayer. Continental countries, however, had adopted a quite different method of agricultural support. They subsidized agriculture not through taxation but through guaranteed prices, which meant that their food prices were higher than those on the world market. In Britain, the taxpayer paid for agricultural subsidies. On the Continent, the consumer paid. The conservative and Catholic parties of the right in France, Germany, and Italy, in power for much of the early postwar period, relied heavily on the votes of peasant farmers, who sought subsidies but resisted high direct taxation. During the early 1960s, the percentage of public revenue raised from direct taxation was over twice as much in Britain as in France and Italy. Having naturally embraced the Continental rather than the British conception of agricultural support, the six founding members of the European Communities would hardly be willing to agree to Britain maintaining higher subsidies for its farmers combined with lower prices in the open market for Commonwealth producers at the expense of agricultural exports from Europe, which would then be priced out of the British market.

The Community's Common Agricultural Policy, which came into force in July 1962, was based on two principles. The first was that all members should be treated equally. This meant that Britain could not receive preferential treatment. The second was that members of the Community should be treated differently from and better than outsiders—the principle of Community preference. These principles meant that the Commonwealth could not be given preferential treatment. The Common Agricultural Policy was based on guaranteed high prices for agricultural products in Europe, together with a common external tariff against agricultural products from elsewhere so as to prevent undercutting—and the elsewhere would include the member states of the Commonwealth which had hitherto provided cheap food to Britain. This would cause considerable problems for Britain, not only for economic but also for sentimental reasons, among a public which remembered the support the Commonwealth had given to Britain during two world wars and during the difficult years of austerity after 1945. Support for the multiracial Commonwealth was particularly strong in the opposition Labour Party, and it was a main reason why its leader, Hugh Gaitskell, came out in 1962 against joining the European Communities. He was much influenced by the views of the Indian High Commissioner, who criticised the consequences of entry since they would mean applying a common external tariff on Asian manufactures and would harm the economies of developing countries.[17] But the old Commonwealth was important too; Gaitskell warned in a party political broadcast in May 1962, 'To go in on bad terms which really meant the end of the Commonwealth would be a step which I think we would regret all our lives and for which history would not forgive us.'[18]

The Common Agricultural Policy meant, then, that cheap food imports from the Commonwealth would have to end. For a member state to enjoy special commercial advantages in other parts of the world would violate the principle of the Communities. Besides, some on the Continent argued, why should they make special provision for New Zealand farmers who were richer than French or Italian peasants? So the Commonwealth, like other countries outside the Common Market, would be subject to levies to prevent its goods from undercutting Community agricultural goods, whose prices would be kept artificially high. There would therefore be a reverse preference against the Commonwealth and in favour of European suppliers. As the president of the Board of Trade, Reginald Maudling, had declared in 1960, 'Our signing the Rome Treaty would involve putting the policy of preferences completely on its head and giving preferences to Europeans instead.'[19] That would, so many believed, threaten the whole concept of the Commonwealth relationship.

It would also mean the end of Britain's traditional cheap food policy. In place of cheap food from the Commonwealth, Britain would be importing more expensive food from the Continent. Instead of the taxpayer subsidising just the small amount of food produced in Britain, British consumers would be subsidizing food from wherever it was produced—whether in Britain, other member states of the Community, or the outside world. That, many feared, would mean a rise in the cost of living—although, in the event, for a short time, food prices actually fell slightly after British entry in 1973 since world food prices rose above the level of European Community prices. Supporters of British entry into the Communities hoped that the rise in the cost of food would be compensated for by access for British industrial goods to the markets of the Six. But the rise in the cost of living would cause wage demands, which would lead to increases in the prices of British products. In addition, British industrial goods would also face increased competition from Continental goods, and it was by no means clear that they could cope with such competition. So the benefits to British industry seemed somewhat speculative and difficult to quantify.

Britain's position worsened during the negotiations in the early 1960s. During the period of negotiation, the six founding members of the Communities came to an agreement on budgetary policy. This agreement was to answer the question, what was to happen to the levies collected on agricultural products? Britain hoped that these would remain with the member state that collected them. But that was not the solution reached by the Six. They decided that if national economies benefited from levies, there would be an incentive to import food from outside rather than from members of the Communities. Therefore the whole of the product of the levies should go to an Agricultural Guidance and Guarantee Fund in Brussels, which would pay it out to producers to subsidise agricultural exports. The money would then be distributed to the member states in proportion to the size of their agricultural sectors. That of course would very much disadvantage Britain, with its small agricultural sector. France, which produced a high proportion of its own food, would pay small levies, Britain large ones. Britain would in effect be financing Continental food imports at the expense of those from the Commonwealth. Money that had previously gone to Australia, Canada, and New Zealand would now go to less efficient farmers on the Continent.

It is therefore hardly surprising that in 1977, four years after Britain eventually entered the Community, it was found that the country was the second largest net contributor after Germany, although at that time only two member states had a lower level of national product per head. The problem of Britain's excessive net contribution caused endless trouble from the time of British entry, and did not come near to resolution until Margaret Thatcher succeeded, after difficult negotiations, in securing a rebate for Britain in 1984. But even after that, disputes about the appropriate level of contribution continued. While Britain could veto any alteration in the calculation of the rebate, its isolation on this issue was to weaken its bargaining position in other negotiations. The relatively large amount of the British contribution later featured strongly in the 2016 referendum campaign.

Britain, then, would find it difficult simply to accept the Treaty of Rome, the founding document of the Communities, and to sign, as it were, on the dotted line. No British government could do this. British governments were forever hoping to be able to amend the rules to bring them more in line with British interests. Many postwar British politicians have felt that their concerns should have priority and that it was the duty of the other member states to help Britain out of its difficulties. They were then constantly being taken by surprise to discover that the European Community has its own interests which may not coincide with those of Britain. On 22 June 2016, the day before the Brexit referendum, *Time* magazine printed the answer Charles de Gaulle gave to a question put to him by Britain's foreign secretary, George Brown, in 1967 in a vain attempt to persuade him to lift his veto on British entry. How, Brown asked, should we solve the problem of Europe? De Gaulle replied, 'There is the Common Market, and for us, there is no problem. For you, there is one: you want to get in, and that is your problem.' No doubt similar thoughts exercised the minds of some European Union leaders during the Brexit process.

In the negotiations for British entry, the Six were determined not to amend the rules to suit Britain's interests, but instead to preserve the institutional structure they had so painfully created. They believed that in the Treaty of Rome, they had achieved, after complex negotiations, an agreement amongst themselves. Britain had not chosen to take part in the process. Now it wanted the rules altered to suit its interests. It was understandable if the Six took the view that they would not, as it were, untie the package. In their view, it was now for

Britain to decide whether to accept the package or not. They hoped that it would, but would not despair if it did not. Britain was negotiating from a position of weakness. Officials warned that no special terms were available. Ministers took no notice.[20] Britain tended to think that the terms of entry should result from a negotiation in which both sides—Britain and the Six— would compromise, with the solution lying halfway between the demands of the two sides; on the Continent, however, the problem was seen as one of fitting Britain into a system that already existed and could not be fundamentally altered. A senior civil servant, Sir Frank Lee, was asked to write a paper for the Cabinet in 1960, and he reported presciently that 'Britain would have to pay a high price to enter. We shall not get the solution we want on the cheap. . . . Therefore, we shall have to be prepared to pay for the sort of settlement we want—in political terms of inconvenience for or damage to some of our cherished interests[, including] the Commonwealth, domestic agriculture, our tariff policy, perhaps indeed our political pride and sense of self-reliance.'[21]

This warning too went unheeded. Indeed, the term 'negotiation,' used for Britain's successive attempts to enter the European Community, is in a sense a misnomer, as it has been for the other countries which have sought to join the European Community or the European Union. The process is characterised by the Europeans determining their own common position and then presenting their proposal to the candidate member. It is then for the candidate member to decide whether to accept the proposal or to withdraw the application. The same has largely been true of the Brexit 'negotiations.' The European Union has presented its agreed position to the departing state, which then has the alternative of accepting it or leaving without a deal, something which many in Britain, though not all, believed would be thoroughly disadvantageous. If one wants to join a tennis club, it is not sensible to quibble about the rules. If one intends to leave but still hopes to use the tennis courts, i.e., to maintain frictionless trade with the E.U., one has very little leverage.

The future, admittedly, would prove that the elements of the Community least favourable to Britain could be altered, first by the Fontainebleau Agreement of 1984, which modified Britain's financial contribution, and then by developments in the European budget itself. During the 1960s and 1970s, when Britain was negotiating to join the European Community, the Common Agricultural Policy was the Community's main common policy, absorbing around 75 percent of its budget and going primarily to direct payments to farmers. Since then, however, the policy has been radically reformed and now accounts for only around 33 percent of the budget, and it is due to fall in the near future to around 30 percent. The main budget item now is aid to the formerly Communist member states in Central and Eastern Europe, which absorbs around 35 percent. This means that there is no longer the same gross mismatch between benefits and contributions as there was when Britain joined. Indeed, most of the richer member states are now net contributors to the budget of the European Union, so its financial system was not as unfavourable to Britain in 2016 as it had been in 1973. Nevertheless, British taxpayers and consumers still see the Common Agricultural Policy as an unfair burden.

In the 1960s, surveys showed that public opinion seemed broadly supportive. But this was to some extent misleading. When faced with specific terms, the public became sceptical, if not downright hostile. A poll carried out in 1966, for example, showed that 66 percent favoured entry. But, when asked if they would still favour entry if it put up the price of food by 2 shillings per pound, only 39 percent were in favour. If entry meant weakening Britain's ties with the Commonwealth, only 25 percent were in favour, and if it meant that New Zealand agriculture 'would suffer quite a bit, only 23 percent were in favour. So membership was acceptable only when it was presented in general terms.

When he announced his decision to join, Macmillan called it a 'turning-point.' But it was not a 'decision for Europe' in the sense of a whole-hearted commitment. British governments sought the minimal adjustment possible. Many still hoped, as perhaps they do today, for a free-trade Europe associated with the Commonwealth and the United States. They did not want the closer ties of the customs union, still less the 'ever closer union' of the Treaty of Rome. Those who wanted Britain to join the European Communities in 1973 accepted that some of its programmes might not be in the country's interest. But they rightly insisted that the cost would be a comparatively small proportion of Britain's budget—around 1 percent of GDP. And this cost, so they argued, would be counterbalanced by the United Kingdom's access to European industrial markets. There would be what were then called 'dynamic' effects. But the trouble was that these dynamic effects were highly uncertain. They were possible but by no means assured—the large budgetary contributions, however, were certain. Further, the 'dynamic' effects to be hoped for by British entry into Continental industrial markets might be counterbalanced by the free entry of the products of the Continental member states, particularly Germany, with its powerful industrial base, into British markets.

There was, so an official historian of Britain's membership of the European Communities has noticed, 'one common thread' in Britain's approach to Europe from the 1960s to the end of the 1980s. It was that 'every one of Britain's Prime Ministers from Macmillan to Thatcher believed, essentially, in an intergovernmental European Community.' 'With rare exceptions,' the same historian concludes, 'the decision to seek membership of the Community and the subsequent experience of that membership, were affairs of the head rather than the heart.'[22]

Ironically, Britain's conception of an intergovernmental Europe had much in common with the Gaullist conception. Every British prime minister would have agreed with de Gaulle in rejecting the idea of a supranational much less a federal Europe. They agreed that Europe should develop as what de Gaulle called a *Europe des états* (he apparently did not use the phrase *Europe des patries*). Indeed, according to Alan Milward, another official historian of Britain's relationship with Europe, Macmillan had told de Gaulle shortly after negotiations began on 25 November 1961 that 'he and his friends in the European Movement had met with great difficulties because they had to battle against the ideas of the Federalist movements which were unrealistic and had no appeal in this country.' That was an exaggeration. There were few federalists in Britain, then or now. But, so Macmillan continued, 'progress was possible towards a united Europe based not on integrationist ideas but on confederal ideas.'[23] So the British and the French agreed on a Europe of states. But they could not agree on whether Britain should be part of it.

One crucial reason for de Gaulle's hostility to Britain was the French fear that if the British entered the Community before the Common Agricultural Policy was finalised, they would seek to sabotage or dilute it. In that case, French agriculture could be ruined. Jean Monnet believed that agriculture had been the fundamental issue which had led to the breakdown of the negotiations in 1963.[24] But perhaps even more fundamental was that the British and the French had quite different conceptions of Europe. For de Gaulle, the central concept was independence. He sought a European Europe, a separate power bloc independent of the United States. At a press conference in 1967, he declared:

> The idea, the hope which, from the beginning, led the Six continental countries to unite was undoubtedly to form an entity that would be European in

all respects, that is to say, that it would not only carry its own weight in trade and production, but that it would be capable one day of dealing politically with anyone, for its own sake and on its own. In view of the special relations of the British with America, together with the advantages as well as the liabilities arising for them out of these relations, in view of the existence of the Commonwealth and of the privileged relations they have with it ... it is not possible to see how the policies could merge, unless the British resumed complete freedom of action, particularly with regard to defence, unless the peoples of the continent gave up the idea of ever building a European Europe.[25]

The British, de Gaulle insisted, must choose between Europe and America. He told Macmillan in June 1962, 'the thought of choosing between Europe and America is not yet fully developed in your mind.'[26] It was not fully developed because the British saw no need to make such a choice.

For Macmillan, by contrast with de Gaulle, the key concept was interdependence. In an entry in his diary for 9 August 1958, he wrote: 'We had seen the old Empire fade away into a new concept. Independence was over; interdependence must take its place.'[27] Interdependence indeed was to be the leitmotif of his administration. Macmillan sought to put Britain at the centre of an interdependent Commonwealth and an interdependent Western Europe while retaining all the rights of a sovereign state, especially in nuclear defence. Like almost every British prime minister, with the sole exception perhaps of Edward Heath, Macmillan saw Britain as a bridge between Europe and America. But this, for de Gaulle, meant diluting the concept of a European Europe.

Macmillan tried to win over de Gaulle with the idea of nuclear cooperation between France and Britain. But this gift was not in Macmillan's control. It required the Americans to share their nuclear secrets with France as they already did with Britain; and in any case, de Gaulle was not interested. He was determined to develop a genuinely French nuclear deterrent—a *force de frappe*—not dependent on any other country. In December 1962, Macmillan, having at last secured American approval, offered de Gaulle the Polaris missile. But if the French accepted, they would have to rely on American nuclear warheads, for they had no nuclear-powered submarines to deliver the missile. And unlike Britain, they were also not yet able to manufacture nuclear warheads. The discussions over nuclear weapons revealed a fundamental difference between Britain and France which Macmillan did not wholly comprehend. For Macmillan, the British nuclear deterrent had the aim of strengthening *interdependence* with America. France, on the other hand, saw its nuclear deterrent as an aid to becoming more *independent* of America. Macmillan's offer, de Gaulle told the French ambassador in London, was 'only a method for enabling the British to observe and possibly to intervene in our nuclear domain on behalf of the Americans.'[28]

The Cuban missile crisis of October 1962 reinforced de Gaulle's view that the United States did not regard defence of Europe as a first priority and might prefer a bilateral settlement with the Soviet Union at Europe's expense. In the 1963 press conference at which he pronounced his veto of Britain's membership in the Communities, de Gaulle mentioned the Cuba crisis four times. So, ironically, Macmillan's offer of nuclear cooperation made de Gaulle even more determined to reject Britain! And Macmillan perhaps never appreciated how weak Britain had become. After his meeting with Macmillan at Rambouillet in December 1962, the French president told his minister for information, 'England's back is broken.'[29]

In December 1962, de Gaulle summed up his objections to British entry at a meeting of his Council of Ministers. He made it clear that agriculture was fundamental.

> If Great Britain and . . . the Commonwealth enter, it would be as if the Common Market had . . . dissolved within a large free trade area. . . . Always the same question is posed but the British don't answer. . . . To please the British, should we call into question the Common Market and the negotiation of the agricultural regulations that benefit us? All this would be difficult to accept. . . . Britain continues to supply itself cheaply in Canada, New Zealand, Australia etc. . . . What will we do with European, and particularly French surpluses? If we have to spend 500 billion [francs] a year on agricultural subsidies what will happen if the Common Market can no longer assist us? These eminently practical questions should not be resolved on the basis of sentiments. [Macmillan] is melancholy and so am I. We would prefer Macmillan's Britain to that of Labour, and we would like to help him stay in office. But what can I do? Except to sing him the Edith Piaf song, 'Ne pleurez pas, Milord.'[30]

De Gaulle's veto left Macmillan in despair. 'All our policies at home and abroad are in ruins. . . . European unity is no more; French domination of Europe is the new and alarming feature; our popularity as a Government is rapidly declining.'[31] The fall in British influence had been precipitate and indeed startling. In just eighteen years, Britain's position had declined from being the undisputed leader of Europe to that of a supplicant. France, a country that had been ruined by the war and whose recovery had been dependent on Britain and America, was now the dominant power on the Continent. It was a stunning reversal of influence. De Gaulle, however, was unmoved. 'Strange times, gentlemen,' he told his Council of Ministers, 'when one cannot say without provoking I do not know what kind of hullaballoo that England is an island and that America is not Europe.' When a former French prime minister, Paul Reynaud, wrote to de Gaulle accusing him of ingratitude in view of Britain's role as an ally of France in two world wars, he received in reply an empty envelope on which was written on the outside, 'Redirect to Agincourt (Somme) or Waterloo (Belgium).'[32]

Little had altered by 1973, when Britain finally joined the European Community. Britain still had to make a decision in principle whether to join what was by now a fully functioning organisation—whether, as it were, to swallow the medicine whole or not at all. But as we have seen, the arrangements that had suited the six founding members were not necessarily suitable for Britain.

Georges Pompidou, the new president of France, supported British entry but made it clear that it would require a profound change in British thinking. Britain must become what the French called 'communautaire.' That meant accepting the Common Agricultural Policy, which was an essential part of the European project. Many in Britain, so Pompidou declared, wanted a free trade area. But the European Community was not and could not be just a free trade area. It also comprised a customs union with a common tariff. Part of its purpose, as Pompidou told Edward Heath, was the preservation of the French countryside and way of life. For the Christian Democratic parties of the Continent, it was vital to ensure preservation of the peasant community, members of a politically sensible and moderate social class hostile to socialism. Europe should not, in their view, become a wholly urban civilisation. A strong agricultural sector, therefore, was necessary to preserve the equilibrium of French society.[33] So for these Christian Democratic parties of the Continent, the Common Agricultural Policy was not just a piece of institutional machinery but a vital part of their philosophy. This was, no doubt, a fine statement of principles. But it also suited France's national interest, which was not necessarily the same as Britain's. Otto von Bismarck, Germany's chancellor in the latter half of the nineteenth century, is supposed to have declared, 'I have always found the word "Europe" in the mouths of those politicians who wanted from other powers something they did not dare demand in their own name.'[34]

The Common Agricultural Policy had been buttressed since 1966 by France's interpretation of what was called the Luxembourg compromise, which President de Gaulle had insisted upon. This compromise declared that where a member state believed a vital national interest was at stake, it could veto any new development in the Communities. Britain was, in principle, sympathetic to this since it was concerned about the implications of majority voting in Europe and the loss of sovereignty which that entailed. But the compromise also froze further development of the Community so that the Common Agricultural Policy, which benefited France, could not be altered without French consent; while other common policies, which might perhaps be in Britain's interest, could be vetoed by other member states. Britain had hoped, for example, for a European regional policy to help its depressed regions. But that would not be possible unless all the member states agreed to it. They were unlikely to do so since it meant they would have to pay from their own budgets to help the depressed regions. The veto power remained until 1986, when it was removed with passage of the Single European Act, ironically at the insistence of the British government led by Margaret Thatcher. For Britain sought to secure a European internal market—the removal of all non-tariff barriers to trade which, in the modern world, are at least as important as tariffs in constraining trade. But these non-tariff barriers could not be removed if the elimination of each one—and there were over three hundred such barriers—were to be subject to an individual national veto. After 1992, when the internal market was completed, the European Union became, in addition to a free trade area and customs union, a single economic market. This was to be Britain's greatest contribution to the development of European Union.

The Single European Act is quite fundamental to the modern conception of the European Union. It converted what had hitherto been external markets among the members of the Community into a single internal market, parallel perhaps to the creation of such a market in the United States in the nineteenth century. As a corollary, the Act legally guaranteed freedom of movement among European Union member states. And this was, of course, one of the key factors leading British voters to reject continued membership in the referendum of 2016. So, ironically, Britain's most important contribution to the development of European Union was also a key factor in leading to Brexit.

In his memoirs, Edward Heath calls the chapter describing Britain's entry 'Fanfare for Europe.' He regarded entry as 'a wonderful new beginning and a tremendous opportunity for the British people.'[35] Few, however, shared Heath's optimism. Indeed, it is easy to overestimate not only the British people's enthusiasm but even their knowledge of European matters. Around fifteen years ago, I heard a pro-European Labour MP give a lecture in which he reported his experience of canvassing in his North of England constituency. A man approached him and said, 'You're a good chap. I shall vote for you. But I don't like all this Europe, I don't think we should join.' The MP gently reminded him that Britain had been a member of the European Community and European Union for more than thirty years. The reply was, 'Well, isn't that typical of politicians. They never tell you anything'! But the referendum of 2016 played a considerable part in extending knowledge of and interest in European Union affairs.

As de Gaulle's prime minister at the time of the first French veto in 1963, Georges Pompidou had written that the difficulties with Britain were not merely technical but *d'un problem de conception meme du Marche Commun et son avenir* [involved a different understanding of the Common Market and its future].[36] These difficulties were to continue to dog Britain even after entering the European Community in 1973. Unfortunately, Britain joined at a time when the *trente glorieuses*—the thirty years of rapid postwar growth—were coming to an end, thanks in part to the Yom Kippur War in the Middle East and the consequent quadrupling of oil prices, a reaction by the Arab states to continued Israeli occupation of their territories. This undermined European solidarity, since some of the member states of the Community supported the Arabs while others supported the Israelis. But even more important, it ended the association of ideas between European integration and prosperity. The long boom was coming to an end, and the European idea was becoming associated with economic difficulties, undermining an incipient British loyalty to Europe which might have been stronger had Britain joined in 1963 as Harold Macmillan had wished.

By 1967, Harold Wilson's Labour government had also become converted to the European cause and made a second application to join the Community, but this was also unsuccessful. It seemed, however, that there was now a domestic consensus on Europe—for all three British political parties were in favour of entry, in principle. But public opinion began to recoil after the second veto in 1967—understandably, no doubt, after two rebuffs. The high point of support for Europe had come in 1966, when more than two-thirds of those sampled favoured British entry. By 1970, 70 percent were against, while 80 percent believed prices would rise more rapidly if Britain joined, and 62 percent wanted a referendum before Britain joined.[37]

Part of the reason for this movement of opinion, no doubt, was a feeling of humiliation after two previous applications to join had been rejected. And by the late 1960s, with all three parties in favour of entry, it was coming to appear that Europe was an issue dividing the political class from the people. The European issue was coming to have explosive potential. Ominously, one leading Conservative politician—Enoch Powell, who had supported the applications in 1961 and 1967—began to campaign against entry with great fervour and eloquence. Powell sought, by combining the issues of Europe and immigration, to create a new popular coalition around the theme of British—or even English—patriotism or nationalism, to restore the nation's wounded pride and self-confidence. He was exploiting a hostility to the political class—which has persisted in one form or another since the 1960s, except perhaps during the Thatcher years. Powell was the first postwar exponent in Britain of something that is now all too familiar—populism. The clash between a political establishment, broadly in favour of Europe, and the people, moving against entry, was to keep Europe a subject of controversy even after entry was secured in 1973.

In addition, the seeming consensus among the parties did not endure. In January 1972, when prime minister Edward Heath signed the Treaty of Accession in Brussels, the opposition leader, Harold Wilson, declined to attend. Labour was coming out in opposition to British entry on 'Tory terms,' even though these terms closely resembled those which Wilson himself had sought when in government. But in opposition, Wilson's leadership was threatened by a left wing which regarded the European Community as a capitalist cartel, and Wilson felt that he could retain his position only by opposing entry and promising a referendum when Labour returned to power. So it was that in 1975 Britain would hold its first ever national referendum, a device that until then was considered quite unconstitutional, on the question of whether the country should remain in the European Community.

The 1975 referendum, pressed upon the Labour leadership by the party's Eurosceptic wing, seemed ironically to confound the Eurosceptics, since the result favored Britain's continued membership in the Community, by a majority of two to one. Some interpreted this outcome as indicating British acceptance, if not enthusiasm, for the European idea. But the seeming enthusiasm was deceptive. It would, in fact, be a grave mistake to attribute the large majority for remaining in the European Community to enthusiasm for the European ideal. It resulted instead from two other interrelated factors. The first was fear. Britain's economic situation was at that time parlous. Inflation was running at 26 percent, the highest it has ever been, unemployment was rising, and trade union power seemed to be a serious threat to the stability of the British polity. One of Britain's European commissioners, Sir Christopher Soames, a former Cabinet minister and ambassador to France, declared that 'This is no time for Britain to be considering leaving a Christmas club, let alone the Common Market.'[38] Opponents of British membership would say that this attitude reflected an unwarranted loss of national self-confidence, an unjustified fear that Britain would be unable to resolve its economic problems without help from the Continent. Nevertheless, fear engendered a feeling that to leave the European Community would be a leap in the dark. One poll showed that 51 percent, including one-third of those voting for Britain to remain in the European Community, thought Britain had been wrong to enter, but 53 percent believed that to leave would 'lead to an immediate political and economic crisis.'[39]

The second reason for the large majority in favour of remaining in the European Community was a leadership effect. All three party leaders favoured Britain remaining in the Community—so also did those politicians of the centre who were most popular with the public. The only popular politician who opposed entry was Enoch Powell. But he stimulated both enthusiasm and repulsion in equal measures—enthusiasm because of his populist nationalism, repulsion because of his attacks on Commonwealth immigration, attacks which descended on occasion to racist language. Many of the other leaders opposed to Europe could easily be labelled extremists: the Communist Party and the neo-fascist National Front; the trade union leaders, unpopular because they seemed unable to control Britain's then chaotic system of industrial relations; the Reverend Ian Paisley, leader of the fundamentalist Protestants of Northern Ireland; and Sinn Fein, thought to be associated with the terrorists of the IRA[40]—but above all, the left wing of the Labour Party, led by Michael Foot, Tony Benn, and Barbara Castle, the most prominent opponents of Europe apart from Powell. All of the best known pro-European figures had strong positive ratings in the opinion polls. All of the anti-European figures, except for Enoch Powell, had strongly negative ratings. One Conservative commentator remarked, 'What was notable was the extent to which the referendum . . . was not really about Europe at all. It became a straight left versus right battle with the normal dividing line shifting further over than in general elections [since the right wing of the Labour Party was broadly for continued membership]—hence the Labour split and their discomfiture. In all the speeches I made to Conservative audiences the trump card was always "beware of Benn, Foot and Castle".'[41]

The issue came to be seen as one dividing the 'moderates' from the 'extremists'; and once it was seen in this way, those opposed to British membership had little chance. Voters took their cues from their leaders at a time when leaders were trusted rather more than they are today. In a comment on the outcome, *The Economist* wrote, 'the most intriguing question is how far the domination of the No campaign by the more left wing Labour spokesmen brought about the huge pro-market Tory vote that clinched the emphatic majority for Europe.'[42] After the result was known, one of the leaders of the pro-Europeans, Home Secretary Roy Jenkins, rather incautiously declared that the voters had taken 'the advice of people they were used to following.'[43] Which of course left open the question: What would the British people do when they ceased to take the advice of people they were used to following? The answer to that question was given in the second Europe referendum in 2016, when a majority of British voters opted for Brexit.

So the outcome of the 1975 referendum was less a ringing endorsement of Europe, but more an endorsement of those political leaders whose judgments were trusted. Perhaps, as often happens in referendums, the people were answering a different question to the one which they were asked.

The leadership factor interacted with the fear factor. There was fear not only of the economic consequences if Britain left, but fear of the extremist politicians who would stand to benefit. This fear was well expressed by Roy Jenkins at the final rally of the Britain in Europe campaign. For Britain to leave the Community, he declared, would be to go into 'an old people's home for fading nations. . . . I do not think it would be a very comfortable old people's home. I do not like the look of some of the prospective wardens.'[44] Perhaps the outcome of the 2016 referendum bears out his warning!

Jenkins was suggesting that the beneficiaries would be nationalists of both left and right, and that Britain would not benefit under their rule. Prime Minister Harold Wilson felt the same, that a victory for the anti-Europeans would empower the wrong kind of people in Britain: the far left and the far right, nationalist, protectionist, xenophobic and backward-looking.

It was difficult to argue, therefore, that the referendum showed enthusiasm for the European enterprise. Negative reasons were of greater importance. A leading opinion pollster working for the Remainers declared: 'Apart from the leadership effect the main factors underpinning the present majority in favour of continued membership form a vague amalgam of caution and conservatism. . . . We have not managed to generate much enthusiasm or to appeal successfully to more idealistic motives.'[45] Two political scientists declared that the verdict of the referendum was 'unequivocal but it was also unenthusiastic. Support for membership was wide but it did not run deep.'[46] The referendum was a vote for the status quo. It was not an expression of confidence in Britain's membership of the European Union but fear of what might happen if Britain were to leave.

But in the referendum, there was a dog that did not bark. In Norway in 1972 a referendum had been held on whether that country should join the European Community. As in Britain, the main parties were in favour, but Norwegians nevertheless rejected membership. That was primarily due to an anti-establishment grass-roots movement against the Community insisting that the pro-Europeans constituted a political class which 'the people' should oppose. In Norway there was a clear populist alternative to the leadership of the established politicians. The obvious question arises—why did no similar populist alternative develop in Britain? Both Tony Benn in the

Labour Party and Enoch Powell, whose following was strongest among working-class voters, sought to arouse such a patriotic and anti-establishment vote. Enoch Powell wrote, on the Sunday before the referendum:

> In Thursday's referendum the British people are deciding if they want to put their shirt on the Common Market—and not only their shirt but the shirts of future generations as well. As they stand wondering, and turning it over, in their minds, a whole crowd of touts come up and say to them—'Look, mates, you know nothing about all this. It's much too complicated for you to understand.' The touts add 'You must take the advice of the people who know best—the Conservative Party; the big industrialists; the CBI; the National Farmers Union, above all, Ted Heath. Take their tip. Do what they tell you. Vote to stay in.' So let's look at the record of these people who 'know best'; who can tell you what will be good for Britain, not just this year or next year but for generations to come. We discover that these are the very people who have always been wrong. Not one horse they have tipped has ever won.[47]

It is a puzzle perhaps that this appeal did not prove more popular, given Britain's economic difficulties and political disaffection which these difficulties were causing. It was that very appeal that was to prove popular in the very different circumstances of the second Europe referendum of 2016. This second referendum was to take place in an atmosphere of rising distrust in political leaders following the 2008 recession and the parliamentary expenses scandal of 2009. During the 2016 referendum,

Nigel Farage managed to convert the United Kingdom Independence Party, of which he was the leader, into the same kind of nationalist populist movement which had swung the 1972 vote in Norway but had been absent in Britain in 1975, and he succeeded in securing a majority for Britain's exit from the European Union.[48]

The referendum of 1975 legitimised British membership of the European Communities. It seemed to settle the issue for good. On the day after the vote, Prime Minister Harold Wilson declared:

> The verdict has been given by a bigger vote, by a bigger majority than has been received by any government in any general election. Nobody in Britain or the wider world should have any doubt about its meaning. It was a free vote without constraint, following a free democratic campaign, conducted constructively and without rancour. It means that fourteen years of national argument are over. It means that all those who have had reservations about Britain's commitment should now join wholeheartedly with our partners in Europe and our friends everywhere to meet the challenge, confronting the whole nation.[49]

Opponents of membership also believed the issue had been settled. Tony Benn from Labour's left declared: 'I have just been in receipt of a very big message from the British people. I read it loud and clear. By an overwhelming majority the British people have voted to stay in and I am sure everybody would want to accept that.'[50] One respected journalist wrote on the day after the referendum: 'The Common Market issue is settled. By their unambiguous vote—the most overwhelming expression of popular will, certainly since 1931—the voters have solved the politicians' dilemmas for them, and banished the issue from the centre of British politics ... secession is now politically inconceivable in this generation.' 'By a clear majority,' the *Sunday Times* declared, 'the British people have declared themselves to be Europeans.'[51]

But these prognostications proved false. The 1975 referendum did not finally settle the issue of Britain's place in Europe. By September 1976, just fifteen months after the referendum, more poll respondents thought membership 'a bad thing' than thought it 'a good thing.' In 1979, just four years after the referendum, survey evidence suggested that a five-to-two majority of the public believed that membership in the European Community had been harmful to Britain.[52] And in 1980, Tony Benn argued that Britain should leave the European Community without a further referendum, a policy adopted by the Labour Party in its 1983 election manifesto. So the referendum settled the European issue only for a very short period.

In 1975, an adviser to the Labour prime minister Harold Wilson declared that Edward Heath had taken the British Establishment into Europe by securing parliamentary consent for entry, but that it had needed Harold Wilson to take the British people into Europe by securing popular consent for entry.[53] In 2016, when the second referendum was held, the British establishment was still committed to Europe. The leaders of all the major parties once again recommended a 'Remain' vote, but this time the British people did not take their advice. As the referendum outcome showed, they were no longer committed to Europe.

3

Brexit Means Brexit
Britain Out of Europe

Britain's membership of the European Community, beginning in 1973, yielded economic benefits in the form of access to a larger market, and after the Single European Act of 1985, in terms of inward investment. After the effects of the Yom Kippur War in the Middle East and the resulting oil crisis had worked themselves out, the years from 1985 until the recession of 2008 were, for the European Union, golden years. Britain in particular, with its large services sector, benefited from the development of the internal market and the removal of non-tariff regulations on goods and services.

But there were, nevertheless, problems with Britain's membership almost from the start. The long and complex battle over what many in Britain saw as their country's excessive budgetary contribution was not resolved until 1984, at the European Council meeting at Fontainebleau. After that came the problem of whether Britain should join the European Monetary System, linking together the currencies of the member states in order to prevent fluctuations between them and assist trade. This system, established in 1979, was intended as a prelude to the creation of a common currency, the euro. The issue of whether Britain should join divided the Conservative cabinet in the late 1980s. Margaret Thatcher was against it, but her leading ministers, the foreign secretary and later leader of the House of Commons and deputy prime minister, Sir Geoffrey Howe, and two of her chancellors, Nigel Lawson and John Major, who was to succeed her as prime minister, were in favour.[1] Gradually the supporters of entry wore Thatcher down, and Britain entered the Exchange Rate mechanism of the European Monetary System in October 1990, just weeks before her downfall in November, which was also precipitated by a European issue—ironically, by her insistence that Britain would never join the euro.

During the 1980s, party allegiances towards Europe shifted. Hitherto, Labour had been the more Eurosceptic party, believing that an integrated Europe would inhibit the development of socialism in one country. That is still the view of a small number of the Left in the Labour Party; sadly for pro-Europeans, that small number included the party's leader, Jeremy Corbyn, and his allies who did their best to inhibit the pro-European sentiments of the majority of Labour MPs and party members. But Labour began to swing towards greater sympathy to the European cause in the late 1980s under the modernising leadership of Neil Kinnock, whose period as leader may be regarded as a prelude to the so-called 'New Labour' era of Tony Blair after 1994. The Labour Party came to believe that the European Community, far from being antagonistic to its aims, might actually assist them. In 1988, the president of the European Commission, Jacques Delors, made a speech to the Trades Union Congress in which he declared that many of the policies sought by the trades unions, policies rejected by Thatcher's neoliberal Conservative government, could be achieved through the European Community. Delors, a former Socialist minister of finance in France, insisted that Europe had a social dimension as well as an economic and political one. Taking as an example its policy of providing protection at work, he declared that 'It is impossible to build Europe on only deregulation. The internal market should be designed to benefit each and every citizen of the Community. It is therefore necessary to improve workers' living and working conditions, and to provide better protection for their health and safety at work.'

This speech helped to secure Labour support for the European cause. But it had the perhaps more serious disadvantage of alienating Margaret Thatcher and many in her Conservative government. Just a few weeks later, Thatcher responded to Delors in her Bruges lecture of 1988, a lecture which has since gained iconic status among Eurosceptics. In this lecture she declared that the European Community had changed for the worse since the Treaty of Rome was signed in 1957. The treaty, she said, had been 'intended as a charter for economic liberty,' but that philosophy was now being undermined by the development of monetary union and proposals for a common currency, and also by proposals of the kind that Delors was advocating for his social Europe. 'We have not,' she declared, 'successfully rolled back the frontiers of the state in Britain, only to see them reimposed at a European level, with a European super-state exercising a new dominance from Brussels.' The Delors speech had convinced her that European integration meant socialism—a mirror image of the earlier view of the Labour left, which had seen European integration as domination by the free market, that it was a neoliberal project. She was arguing that it meant domination by government, that it was in essence a socialist project. Perhaps both were wrong.

Although Eurosceptics welcomed the Bruges speech, Thatcher insisted she was not anti-European. 'Britain,' she said, ' does not dream of some cosy, isolated existence on the fringes of the Community. Britain's destiny is in Europe, a part of the

Community.' Indeed, if one rereads the speech today, it can seem positively pro-European. She called, for example, for stronger defence and foreign policy cooperation among member states. She also insisted, just a year before the collapse of the Berlin Wall, that 'we shall always look on Warsaw, Prague and Budapest as great European cities.' The speech prefigured her support for the enlargement of the European Union to include the formerly Communist states, an enlargement largely completed in 2004. Indeed, the two major contributions made by Britain to Europe were the single market and enlargement, both in large part due to Margaret Thatcher. Yet British political leaders were not prepared to take the credit for these constructive achievements. And the more pro-European parts of the Bruges lecture made little impact. That was because the real significance of the speech was that it represented the first frontal attack on what might be called the Community method of integration—the Monnet or Schuman method. Margaret Thatcher was opposing the idea of supranationality and the sharing of sovereignty. Europe, she believed, should instead develop through intergovernmental cooperation, 'willing and active cooperation between independent sovereign states.' Nation-states, she insisted, were 'intractable political realities which it would be folly to seek to override or suppress in favour of a wider but as yet theoretical European nationhood.' She offered, therefore, an alternative intergovernmental vision of Europe—a Gaullist vision of a *Europe des états*. That view was in many respects prescient. Thatcher's view of Europe also came to be espoused to some extent by the German chancellor Angela Merkel in her own Bruges lecture of 2010—as important as Thatcher's address but less frequently quoted—in which she too emphasised the intergovernmental rather than the integrationist method.

Two years before delivering her Bruges lecture, Thatcher had helped to make Britain's most important single contribution to the development of Europe, the Single European Act of 1986, perhaps the most important of all the amendments to the Treaty of Rome. This act provided for a single internal market in goods and services and led to qualified majority voting in the Council of Ministers, so ending the Luxembourg Compromise, which had seemed to require unanimity. The act was integrationist, yet Thatcher championed it because she believed that it was in Britain's interest. But the preamble to that act refers to another ambition of the European Union—the 'progressive realisation of European Monetary Union.' To that ambition Thatcher was resolutely opposed. This did not, however, prevent her from signing the act, and she voiced no objection at the time. What was her motive? In her memoirs, she does not resort to the easy excuse of saying that she was deceived by her officials. Instead, she declares: 'I had one overriding positive goal. This was to create a single Common Market. . . . The price which we would have to pay to achieve a Single Market with all its economic benefits, though, was more majority voting in the Community. There was no escape from that, because otherwise particular countries would succumb to domestic pressures and prevent the opening-up of their markets. It also required more power for the European Commission: but that power must be used in order to create and maintain a Single Market, rather than to advance other objectives.'²

Thatcher believed that qualified majority voting should be restricted to matters connected with the creation of the single market. It should not be used for other matters such as, for example, taxation policy. But this was not the view of the other member states, or of Jacques Delors. They saw it as a move towards a more integrated continent, to be achieved through harmonisation. Moreover, they also believed that the extension of the free market should be accompanied by a social Europe to ensure protection for those whose bargaining power was weak or nonexistent. As a beginning to the process of creating a social Europe, therefore, the Single European Act also introduced qualified majority voting on measures dealing with the health and safety of workers, a policy which Margaret Thatcher strongly but unavailingly resisted.

Thatcher regarded the single market as a kind of World Trade Organisation arrangement for non-tariff barriers, an extension of a free trade agreement. But as Americans discovered over a hundred years ago, a single internal market needs political and juridical regulation. It requires, for example, effective competition law if the market is to be effectively policed. It is therefore not possible to make Thatcher's distinction between a single market and integration. The single market *requires* integration. And on the Continent, integration, far from being deplored, was welcomed as a step towards greater European unity. So, while Thatcher believed that a choice had to be made between a free economy and greater regulation, most Europeans thought both were necessary, and that the task was to find a balance between them. For Thatcher's opponents in the Conservative Cabinet, the real issue was not whether there ought to be more integration, but what *shape* and *form* that integration should take, and whether Britain would get to play a part in helping to decide that shape and form, or would instead remain on the sidelines—for there are of course many nuances to the notion of integration, as Americans are so well aware.

Jacques Delors, the president of the European Commission, believed, with French president François Mitterrand and a number of other European leaders, that the logic of the single market entailed monetary union and a common currency, so as to eliminate barriers to trade caused by national currency fluctuations. That, they believed, was particularly important given the breakdown in 1971 of the Bretton Woods fixed exchange rate system after the abandonment by President Nixon of gold convertibility of the dollar. The Exchange Rate Mechanism and later the single currency were seen as ways of protecting Europe from the damage which, so it was believed, would be caused by floating exchange rates and competitive devaluations. The first step in this enterprise was to create a European Monetary System of fixed exchange rates as a zone of monetary stability in Europe. Exchange rate stability, Delors believed, was necessary for the common price system of the Common Agricultural Policy to be effective, to encourage trade between member states, and above all to give Europe more weight in a world economy dominated by a volatile U.S. dollar. For this reason, a European system of fixed exchange rates, and indeed monetary union, had long been an aim of the European Community—since 1969, in fact, before Britain became a member. Some British Conservatives supported this first step towards monetary union, though most were opposed to the single currency, because they believed that membership in the European Monetary System would help to control inflation in Britain by locking Britain in to the monetary discipline of the European Community, dominated as it was by Germany with its strong belief in monetary stability.

Margaret Thatcher, however, had come to believe that fixed exchange rates were a mistake, since they led to market distortion. In her view, the Exchange Rate Mechanism was an attempt to control the market, and so went against economic rationality. It sought to yoke together two very different economies—the British and the German—but what was right for Germany might not be right for Britain. There was some danger, given Germany's strong economy, that British economic policy might be determined not by what was in Britain's interests, but by what was in Germany's interests or by an economic standard that Britain could not match. One of Thatcher's favourite aphorisms was that if you try to buck the market, the market will buck you.

The development of the European Community, therefore, gave rise to two concerns on Thatcher's part. The first was that it was emphasising harmonisation and integration, so weakening national sovereignty; the second was that it was tending to extend rather than limit the role of the state. These two elements formed the core of the Thatcherite critique of Europe.

Europe was to be the occasion of Margaret Thatcher's downfall. For her growing Euroscepticism was arousing the ire of her deputy prime minister, Sir Geoffrey Howe, foreign secretary from 1983 to 1989 and then leader of the House of Commons until 1990, when he resigned. In his resignation speech, he declared that the issue of Europe had caused for him a 'tragic conflict of loyalties with which I have myself wrestled for perhaps too long.'[3] Indeed, he entitled his memoirs *Conflict of Loyalty*; and on the last page he writes, 'I wanted to change the policies, not the leader. But if that meant the leader had to go, then so it had to be.'[4] A main area of policy conflict had been over the question of whether Britain should join the Exchange Rate Mechanism. Pressure from her senior ministers persuaded Thatcher to join in October 1990, somewhat against her instincts. This decision was very widely supported—by the Labour Party, the Liberal Democrats, and the main employer and trade union organisations, the Confederation of British Industry and the Trades Union Congress. It was opposed by just eleven Conservative MPs and a few from the left wing of the Labour Party.

Some years later, one of Thatcher's allies said, 'When Margaret Thatcher is dead and opened it will be those three letters Exchange Rate Mechanism that will be lying in her heart.'[5] In fact, joining was one of her last significant decisions. Six weeks later, she resigned as prime minister. At an E.U. summit in Rome in October 1990, she declared that the European Community was 'on the way to cloud-cuckoo land' and announced that

Britain would never agree to the single currency, and would indeed seek to veto it—a declaration which she then repeated in the House of Commons, where she added that the Community was 'striving to extinguish democracy' and that monetary union would open the 'back door to a federal Europe.'[6] This was flouting a Cabinet decision. For the Cabinet had agreed that while Britain did not intend to join the single currency in the foreseeable future, entry should not be ruled out in principle. For ruling it out would, in the Cabinet's view, isolate Britain in the European Union. Geoffrey Howe was particularly insistent that such isolation must be avoided and that Britain should not be seen as choosing a different destiny from the vast majority of member states. It would be better, in his view, for Britain to be seen as constructive rather than negative—to be eager to join in European initiatives rather than always seeking to opt out from them.

In his resignation speech, Howe declared that the prime minister's 'perceived attitude towards Europe is running increasingly serious risks for the future of our nation.' His resignation precipitated a leadership challenge which proved fatal to Thatcher, who, out of office, became more Eurosceptic. In her book *Statecraft*, published in 2002, she wrote that Britain's problems in the twentieth century had been caused by Europe but resolved by the Anglo-Saxons, amongst whom she included the Americans! British membership of the European Communities, she went on, had been 'a political error of historic magnitude.' Britain should therefore renegotiate to recover its sovereignty; and if that proved impossible, as it would almost certainly prove to be, it should leave what had become the European Union.[7] Many years later, Nigel Farage, the leader of the United Kingdom Independence Party, declared that were Margaret Thatcher still alive, there would be no need for his party. But Thatcher did not become a Brexiteer until after she had left office.

It is a paradox that Margaret Thatcher, to whom the European Union largely owes Britain's two constructive contributions to the European enterprise, the single market and enlargement, was to turn against Europe in her final years. For the internal market had given Britain considerable economic advantages, helping it to benefit from globalisation. But these benefits were achieved at the expense of a further erosion of national and parliamentary sovereignty. One component of Thatcherism, the development of a free market in Europe, was coming to be polarised against another, national sovereignty. The question was whether Britain was prepared to pay a price in terms of loss of sovereignty to secure the economic benefits of integration, as well as the very real geopolitical and diplomatic benefits in terms of influence that it gained from being a member of the European Union. In some areas, indeed, Britain has played a leading role—for example in climate change negotiations at the Paris 2015 summit, and in telecommunications policy—while E.U. commissioners such as Leon Brittan and Peter Mandelson were at the heart of European Union policy on trade and financial regulation, ensuring that policy in these areas was shaped in a manner advantageous to Britain. But it fell to the post-Thatcher Conservative Party to balance these very real benefits against the loss of sovereignty.

It took a long time for the party to resolve the conflict. Some Conservatives, such as Michael Heseltine, deputy prime minister from 1995 to 1997, and Kenneth Clarke, chancellor of the Exchequer from 1994 to 1997, welcomed integration, but they were largely from an older generation. The majority deplored the loss of sovereignty. Thatcherism, therefore, was becoming an unstable amalgam, but its elements were to some extent contained until 1990. After that, however, opinion polarised. The tension between the two elements of Thatcherism was, no doubt, bound to implode in due course, until, after the

2016 referendum, the Conservatives were to become a Brexit party.

Thatcher's successor as prime minister was her chancellor, John Major. He struck a new note, declaring, in a speech to the Konrad Adenauer Stiftung in March 1991, 'My aim for Britain in the Community can be simply stated. I want to be where we belong. At the very heart of Europe.'[8] In 1992 he successfully negotiated the Maastricht Treaty, which extended the European Union's right of initiative into many new areas of policy, in particular foreign policy and defence, and provided for a common currency, the euro. This marked a sea change in the development of European unity. Major, through skilful negotiation, secured an opt-out for Britain from the social chapter of the treaty, and even more important, from monetary union. Together with Denmark, Britain would be exempt from having to join the eurozone. It would join only if and when Parliament decided to do so.

But Britain's troubles with Europe were by no means over. For membership of the European Monetary System was causing considerable damage to the British economy, a result, in large part, of German reunification. This was proving to be inflationary—since the German chancellor, Helmut Kohl, had chosen a 1:1 exchange rate between the West German Deutschmark and the East German Ostmark, even though the Ostmark was obviously worth much less than the Deutschmark. In addition, Kohl had chosen to finance reunification not by raising taxes but by borrowing. In consequence, Germany had to raise interest rates. Higher interest rates might have been appropriate for Britain in 1990, when still suffering from the effects of a property-fuelled boom. But by 1992, Britain was in recession and needed to reduce interest rates, not to raise them. As Margaret Thatcher had predicted, the Exchange Rate Mechanism was leading not to the convergence of Europe's economies but to divergence—and British economic policy seemed to be determined by what was right for Germany rather than by what was right for Britain. Many argued that the same would happen were Britain ever to join the eurozone.

By the summer of 1992, the markets had come to the view that the British government lacked the resolve to impose the necessary measures of economic and financial discipline needed to sustain continued membership of the Exchange Rate Mechanism. Market judgments proved self-fulfilling, and as Thatcher had predicted, the attempt to buck the market led to Britain being bucked by the market. Britain sought help from the German central bank, the Bundesbank, and from German politicians. Britain did not get it. The Bundesbank refused to lower interest rates more than a token amount, and indeed on the day before Britain left the Exchange Rate Mechanism, the head of the Bundesbank declared that weak currencies might have to be devalued. He did not want the Bundesbank to be tied to a weak pound. Germany believed that the British government should emulate its own financial discipline, which had been the basis of its success. During the discussions with Britain, when Britain's membership of the Exchange Rate Mechanism was under strain, the head of the Bundesbank, Helmut Schlesinger, said to German finance minister Theo Waigel, 'In 1948, remember we had nothing, and look at what we have now. We achieved it by pursuing our own line of policy. We mustn't weaken now.'9

Germany was to be much criticised by British ministers for failing to help. In his autobiography, John Major tells the story of phoning the head of his policy unit, Sarah Hogg, who was on a walking tour of Scotland—this was of course before the days of the internet or mobile phones. She had to go to a police phone to answer the prime minister's call. 'Prime Minister,' she said, 'I don't think we can rely on the Germans.' The two police constables standing nearby, who had overhead, replied without knowing what she was talking about, 'Dead right.' In his memoirs, Major comments that the two constables certainly 'knew what was what in world affairs'![10]

The British criticism, though obviously self-interested, was not wholly without foundation. Admittedly, the Germans seemed to have the perhaps odd idea that they were there to defend German and not British national interests. But there was another aspect to the crisis. Germany had become a hegemonic power within the system, and as such surely had responsibilities which went along with that role. As a hegemonic power, Germany had an obligation, surely, to defend not only the German national interest but also the European interest; and that interest required it to help the British out of their difficulties. The Germans always insisted that they were committed Europeans and that they favoured European solutions to problems. But by a happy coincidence, these European solutions always seemed to be those which suited German national interests. Perhaps Germany after World War II has never really been prepared to accept the obligations that go with the role of hegemon in Europe. The Germans have indeed never appeared comfortable with that role, for obvious historical reasons. Still, the Germans' attitude made them the convenient scapegoat, as the Americans have often been, for what could be seen as British misjudgements, and for Britain's failure to make its economy more competitive.

On so-called Black Wednesday in 1992, which the Eurosceptics were to call White Wednesday, Britain was forced out of the Exchange Rate Mechanism, losing in the process around £3.3 billion net in foreign currency reserves. Approval of the Conservative Party in opinion poll ratings fell from 43 percent to 29 percent and did not recover, even though leaving the European Monetary System did not have the catastrophic consequences that many had predicted. Indeed, it was followed by a period of low inflation, although whether that was a result of leaving remains a matter of dispute amongst economists. Perhaps the controversy is best summed up by Sir Alan Budd, who was chief economic adviser to the Treasury from 1991 to 1997. He wrote in 2005, 'The period of membership of the Exchange Rate Mechanism was not a very worthy episode. A slightly cruel summary of it would be to say that we went into the Exchange Rate Mechanism in despair and left in disgrace. Nevertheless, we are still enjoying the benefits of it.'[11]

But the benefits took some time to arrive. The immediate economic consequences were catastrophic. During the first nine months of 1992, there were nearly 36,000 bankruptcies and nearly 25,000 company liquidations. More than 68,000 properties were repossessed, and over 200,000 property owners found themselves in mortgage payment arrears. GDP growth was negative: −2.2 percent in 1991, and −0.6 percent in 1992. The hardship was felt especially strongly amongst the core Conservative—or Thatcherite—constituency: small businesses and the self-employed. They were devastated by the economic collapse. The repossessions and mortgage arrears seemed to put an end to the Conservative dream of a property-owning democracy.

The political consequences were no less serious. One senior and much respected Conservative back-bencher declared that he had been told by many that departure from the Exchange Rate Mechanism was 'the biggest humiliation for Britain since Suez.'[12] It was a catastrophe for the Major government, ruining the reputation for good economic management that Conservative governments had, on the whole, enjoyed since 1951. It was largely for this reason that the party remained out of power for so long after 1997. In the aftermath of withdrawal, taxes had to be raised, and this prevented the Conservatives from tagging Labour in the 1997 general election, as they had done in 1992, as the party of high taxation. The Conservatives were in addition now tagged as the party of devaluation. Labour, for the first time since the 1970s, was coming to be seen by the voters as more competent in economic affairs than its main opponents. In the 2005 election campaign, the Labour prime minister, Tony Blair, said 'the Conservatives used to run on the economy—now they run away from it.' The Conservatives were not to recover their reputation for nearly twenty years, losing three general elections in the process—those of 1997, 2001, and 2005.

In addition, the debacle further delegitimised the pro-Europeans in the Conservative Party. The Eurosceptics argued that leaving the Exchange Rate Mechanism enabled Britain to devalue and led to economic recovery. That is why they called the day of departure not Black Wednesday but White Wednesday, since it restored to Britain the freedom to make its own economic policy. The debacle made it almost certain that Britain would not join the eurozone. The Eurosceptics pointed out that if Britain were ever to join the euro, it could not devalue—as the Greeks, Italians, and others have discovered. During the Greek eurozone crisis of 2011, Foreign Secretary William Hague was to compare the eurozone to a burning building with no exit. The Eurosceptics in the Conservative Party said that the commitment to Europe was a failed policy of pre-Thatcherite days—a legacy of failed leaders such as Harold Macmillan and Edward Heath. It was an aberration, a departure from true Conservatism, which emphasised not integration but the primacy of the nation. True Conservatives, therefore, must be Eurosceptics. Margaret Thatcher had come to share that view. She declared that the Maastricht treaty was 'a treaty too far,' and in her maiden speech in the House of Lords on 2 July 1992, she argued for a referendum on the treaty and said that, if there were one, she would vote against ratification.

Departure from the Exchange Rate Mechanism began a civil war in the Conservative Party which raged until 2019. At the party's 1992 conference, which was a prelude to the parliamentary debates on ratification of the Maastricht treaty, Foreign Secretary Douglas Hurd reminded the delegates of the disastrous effects of two previous splits in the party—both of which raised equally profound issues of national identity: the split over the Corn Laws in 1846 and the split over tariff reform after 1903. The first had kept the Conservatives out of a majority government for twenty-eight years, the second for seventeen years. 'Let us decide to give that madness a miss,' he pleaded. But his plea fell on deaf ears. Europe was to keep the Conservatives out for thirteen years. John Major himself accepts, in his autobiography, that Black Wednesday was 'a political and economic calamity. It unleashed havoc in the Conservative Party and it changed the political landscape of Britain. On that day, a fifth Conservative victory, which always looked unlikely, unless the opposition were to self-destruct, became remote, if not impossible.'[13]

A former Conservative minister, Norman Tebbit, who had been very close to Margaret Thatcher, called the Exchange Rate Mechanism the 'Eternal Recession Mechanism.' He asked the delegates to the 1992 conference three questions:

Do you want to be citizens of a European Union?
To see a single currency?
To let other countries decide Britain's immigration policy?

Not surprisingly perhaps, he received a loud 'No' from the audience after each of these questions, and a standing ovation at the end of his speech.

The years 1990–92 began the chain of events which led to the Brexit referendum of 2016.

The transformation of Conservative Party attitudes was mirrored by a switch in public opinion. Until 1992, there had been a slow but steady rise in acceptance of U.K. membership of the European Community. Although there had been little positive enthusiasm, there had been what one might call a permissive consensus on Europe. But following departure from the Exchange Rate Mechanism and the crisis over the Maastricht treaty, that consensus collapsed and support for Europe fell. From 1992 until 2015, according to successive surveys by the British Social Attitudes study, there were only six years in which fewer than 50 percent favoured either leaving the European Union or weakening Britain's relationship with it. Although some economists, as we have seen, took the view that membership had been beneficial, it is understandable if the popular view was that Britain had been forced out of a system which did not suit it, and was better off as a result. Therefore, so it seemed, the Eurosceptics were right and the pro-Europeans wrong. Not a single opinion poll in Britain ever showed a majority for joining the euro. The Eurosceptics, therefore, seemed in tune with the British public long before the 2016 referendum.

Under the New Labour and pro-European governments of Tony Blair and Gordon Brown, between 1997 and 2010, the European issue became relatively quiescent. This was in large part because the economy seemed to be flourishing, and so, although the British public was becoming more Eurosceptic, Europe was a less salient issue. When, just before polling day in 2001, the Conservative leader, William Hague, declared that Labour would take Britain into the eurozone and that voters had 'just 24 hours to save the pound,' the voters ignored him. They did not know what he was talking about.

After the general election of 2010, the Labour government of Gordon Brown was replaced with a Conservative/Liberal Democrat coalition led by David Cameron, who had became

Conservative leader in 2005. He had sought to modernise his party. Part of that process of modernisation was to concentrate on issues other than Europe, issues such as the condition of the public services, and particularly the National Health Service, which he regarded as of much greater immediate importance to voters. In his first Party Conference speech as leader in 2006, he declared that he wanted the Conservatives to stop 'banging on' about Europe, to forget about an issue which was dividing the party and which appeared to have so little resonance with the British public.[14] His coalition with the pro-European Liberal Democrats, the first peacetime coalition in Britain since 1931, was possible only because the issue of Europe was very much in the background at this time. Otherwise, the broadly Eurosceptic Conservatives and the pro-European Liberal Democrats would not have been able to reach agreement.

But Europe soon became a salient issue again, largely because of mass immigration from central and eastern Europe following the enlargement of the European Union after 2004 to embrace the formerly communist states. The Single European Act of 1986, which provided for the single internal market, had given a legal guarantee to the four freedoms—goods, capital, services, and persons. No E.U. member state, therefore, could restrict immigration from any other member state. Westminster, although it could restrict immigration from outside the European Union, and in particular from the English-speaking Commonwealth, could not restrict E.U. immigration. Resentment at this difference was a prime motivator of the Leave vote in the British referendum in 2016. The formerly Communist countries had far lower standards of living than almost all of the previous member states, and their people felt a magnetic attraction towards the West, and particularly to Britain, with its developed welfare provisions and National Health Service.

British governments seriously underestimated the quite unprecedented scale of the immigration that ensued. Between 1881 and 1914, around 325,000 Jews had immigrated into Britain from eastern Europe, and another 50,000 came between 1933 and 1939 to escape the Nazis. At the time of the Immigration Act of 1971, which stopped the permanent immigration of workers from the Commonwealth, there were around 600,000 U.K. citizens born in the Commonwealth living in Britain. That included a small number who had come to Britain before 1939. Most, however, had come in the postwar years. In 1972, around 30,000 Ugandan Asians expelled by President Idi Amin were admitted. But there are now around 3.7 million migrants from the European Union living in Britain. So immigration from the European Union has been of a quite different order of magnitude from previous waves, and it could not be controlled by Westminster, unlike immigration from outside the E.U.[15]

Such mass European immigration had not been foreseen in the Treaty of Rome, which had been negotiated in 1957 by six countries of roughly similar living standards, and before the age of cheap mass tourism. The admission of the former Communist countries, in the poorest of which income per head was just over one-fifth of that in Britain, totally altered the situation. Most economists believed that immigration was good for Britain, and indeed Tony Blair's Labour government had encouraged it, to overcome shortages of labour. But in the poorer sections of the country, many felt it to be disadvantageous. For them, immigration seemed primarily to have benefited the elite, who were able to hire Polish builders and Lithuanian au pairs inexpensively. The benefits seemed less obvious to the so-called left behind on low wages, who believed that an unlimited supply of immigrant labour kept wages low, while the benefits in the form of an increase in tax revenues were not obviously visible. Difficulties in the public services—long hospital waiting lists, long waiting times at doctors' surgeries, overcrowded classrooms—were, by contrast, highly visible and were mistakenly attributed to the incursion of immigrants.

In addition, many people living in poorer areas found it difficult to cope with the social effects of immigration, the transformation of their communities which, so they argued, had occurred without their consent, without their having been asked. It seemed to some to undermine the sense of reciprocity which, so they believed, should be the basis of the welfare state. Access to benefits, on this view, should depend on contributions; they should not therefore be available on the same basis to recent immigrants who had not contributed, indeed had not enjoyed the opportunity to contribute. For that would undermine the basis of citizenship, the notion of the community as a joint enterprise among its citizens.

Mass immigration thus created a disconnect between the elite and the people. This disconnect was symbolised in an iconic episode in the 2010 general election campaign. Prime Minister Gordon Brown was campaigning in Rochdale, where he met a Labour voter who told him she was worried about immigration. He gave her a standard defence of the benefits immigration had brought. When he returned to his car, not realising that his microphone was still on, he complained about having been brought face to face with someone he called a 'bigoted woman.' Widely reported on the media, the prime minister's comments did little for his election campaign and confirmed for many working-class voters that the Labour leadership, indeed the political class as a whole, took little interest in the worries of ordinary people and were indeed happy to ignore them. By the time of the referendum in 2016, the public had lost confidence in either party's ability to address the immigration issue.

Concerns about high levels of immigration became particularly prominent after the 2008 recession. In both Europe and America, the financial collapse led to fundamental shifts in political alignments and attitudes, shifts which have by no means yet worked themselves out and which are still being felt. People working for low wages saw their standard of living stagnate, while the better off seemed to have remained untouched. The political and financial elites had appeared less than competent in dealing with the fallout from the crisis, which cast doubt on the neoliberal premise that allowing financiers and bankers to earn large sums of money would benefit the whole community. The financial crisis also led people to question the wisdom of experts, in particular those economists who had assured them that inequalities of income and wealth were beneficial since they would help to raise the standard of living of the less well-off. The experts had been wrong, but it was the less well-off who bore the brunt. It is hardly surprising that the hair-raising predictions of the economic 'experts' as to the consequences of Brexit ended up being largely ignored in the 2016 referendum.

Many on the left had hoped that the financial crisis would prove a social democratic moment, that it would lead to a fundamental change in attitudes toward the free market. They hoped that it would yield a strong electoral constituency for greater regulation of markets and the banks, and in favour of redistributive taxation. The philosophy of market liberalism has certainly taken a beating. In Britain, for example, the Conservative Party's manifesto for the general election of 2017 declared, remarkably, 'We must reject the ideological templates provided by the socialist left and the libertarian right'—thus implicitly equating Margaret Thatcher with the left-wing Labour Party leader, Jeremy Corbyn—'and instead embrace the mainstream view that recognises the good that government can do.' Later the manifesto declared, 'The government's agenda will not be allowed to drift to the right.' Theresa May, the prime minister in 2017, was as far from the neoliberal approach of Thatcherism as Corbyn was from Tony Blair, whose New Labour governments had accepted many of Thatcher's reforms.

But the beneficiary of the weakening of the philosophy of market liberalism was not to be social democracy. Indeed in Britain, as in so much of the Continent, both of the internationalist philosophies associated with economic progress, economic liberalism and social democracy, appeared to be in retreat, with Theresa May reacting against the one, and Jeremy Corbyn reacting against the other. The 2017 election in Britain marked a movement away from the consensus on these two philosophies which had ruled Britain from the time of Margaret Thatcher in the 1980s to the time of David Cameron, who had resigned the premiership in 2016, just after the Brexit referendum. What the financial crisis led to was not a social democratic moment but a nationalist moment. As in much of the Continent and in the United States, it strengthened national feeling while weakening class feeling and social solidarity. The alienation and sense of disfranchisement which arose benefited the right more than the left, as it had done in 1930s Europe, when Marxists had wrongly predicted the collapse of capitalism.

Although the financial crash has on the whole benefited the right, it has given rise to a mood which is radical and anything but conservative. Similar trends were observable on the Continent and in America. On the Continent, the main effect was to weaken parties of the centre in favour of parties of the radical right; although in the Mediterranean countries, the beneficiaries have sometimes been parties of the radical left. The main ideological victims in Europe and in the United States were the internationalist doctrines which had been the governing ideologies for many years—economic liberalism and social democracy. Indeed, the financial crisis may even be said to have inaugurated a crisis of economic and political liberalism. That was bound to have considerable effects on Britain's membership of the European Union.

The financial crisis led to a sea change in the politics of many of the advanced democracies. Until 2008, politics in Britain and in many other democracies had been largely dominated by economics, by arguments over the role of the state in economic affairs. After 2008, however, politics came to be dominated by questions of identity. In Britain, the key question came to be less 'What ought to be the role of state?' than 'What does it mean to be British?'—and in particular, whether being British was compatible with being European and whether being British was compatible with being Scottish. In the 2015 general election in Britain, held just a year before the referendum on the European Union, the only two parties to make substantial gains were UKIP—the United Kingdom Independence Party, dedicated to taking Britain out of the European Union—and the Scottish National Party, dedicated to taking Scotland out of the United Kingdom. Both emphasised issues of identity rather than economics. They complained not that their political opponents were insufficiently left wing or right wing but that they were insufficiently British or insufficiently Scottish.

Concerns about identity seem to have been felt most strongly by the disadvantaged and insecure, the victims of social and economic change, who were alienated from the banking and financial establishment, which seemed to have weathered the crisis with far less difficulty than the left behind. The decline of manufacturing industry had led to a loss of jobs for the less qualified. It was no longer possible, as it had been sixty years ago, for a young person to leave school, move immediately into a job without qualifications, and be confident that he would be able to retain that job for life, that he would never be unemployed. For the semi-skilled and the unskilled, the credit crunch highlighted the bleakness of their employment prospects.

The elite, by contrast, seemed to be in a much stronger position. It was not only socially mobile, benefiting from a meritocratic society, it was also geographically mobile. The elite tended to be located in large conurbations such as London, Manchester, and Newcastle, all of which supported Remain in the 2016 referendum. The elite is internationalist—more comfortable in Brussels than in Blackpool or Burnley. In America, similarly, it is more comfortable in Nassau or Nice than in Nebraska. But those left behind by the decline of manufacturing industry are neither socially nor geographically mobile. They remain rooted to their decaying communities. Remarkably, around 60 percent of the British population live within twenty miles of where they grew up.[16] They do not share the multicultural perspective of Londoners, who welcome immigration and favour the European Union. The contrast between London—the only region of England where a majority voted Remain—and the rest of England may be one of the reasons so many media commentators, based in the capital, missed the significance of the grassroots insurgency in provincial England which led to Brexit. Many of those who voted for Brexit felt that they had been ignored and were angry at the political and economic establishment. The referendum offered an opportunity to display that anger.

The growth of nationalism in Britain, the growth of the sense of Britishness, was bound to have its effect on attitudes towards the European Union, though the effect of course is not easy to measure. What is clear is that shortly after David Cameron's coalition government took office, in 2010, Europe once again became a salient issue. In the general election of 2010, the United Kingdom Independence Party, UKIP, whose main policy platform was Brexit, had secured 3 percent of the vote—nearly a million votes, by far the highest total recorded in modern times by any minor party in Britain not allied to a major party. The near-fascist British National Party, also opposed to E.U. membership, secured another 2 percent—more than Oswald Mosley's British Union of Fascists had ever appeared likely to secure between the wars. Indeed, that party had never been confident enough even to contest seats in a general election.

In 2011, the Cameron coalition established a petition system providing that any petition on a matter of government responsibility which attracted 100,000 signatures would be eligible for a debate at Westminster. The first such petition demanded a referendum on the European Union; the second demanded a curb on immigration. At the same time, a survey by the polling company YouGov showed that four-fifths of the population in England believed that the country was overcrowded.[17]

In October 2011, the House of Commons debated on whether to hold a referendum on Britain's membership of the European Union. Eighty-one Conservative MPs—nearly half of all Conservative MPs not on the government payroll—broke a three-line whip requiring them to support the government's policy of opposing a referendum, and voted in favour of one. Grass-roots pressure on Prime Minister Cameron proved impossible to resist, and in January 2013, in his Bloomberg speech, he committed the Conservatives to 'fundamental reform' of the European Union and then a referendum on whether Britain should remain. Democratic consent for Europe, he declared, was 'now wafer thin.' If the people were not consulted, he believed, it would 'make more likely our eventual exit,' since anti-E.U. feeling would grow and fester. Promising to negotiate a 'new settlement' for Britain in the European Union, Cameron concluded by saying, 'I want the EU to be a success. And I want a relationship between Britain and the EU that keeps us in it. ... If we can negotiate such an arrangement, I will campaign for it with all my heart and soul. Because I believe something very deeply. That Britain's national interest is best served in a flexible, adaptable and open EU and that such a EU is best with Britain in it.' So, once he had secured the right relationship with the European Union, he would campaign for Britain to remain.

His Bloomberg speech was pro-European, though few appreciated it at the time, and Cameron was more successful in his renegotiation than is often thought. In particular he ensured that the rights of the non-eurozone members, which of course included Britain, were protected against the majority of eurozone members, who seemed to be moving towards closer integration through banking union and perhaps even fiscal union. Cameron sought to protect the institutions of the City of London, whose financial institutions brought in considerable tax revenues—but of course the interests of the City could not be brought to the fore in the referendum, since its image had been so tarnished by the financial crisis. 'Vote to Remain in the European Union now that the interests of the City have been protected' would not have made a powerful electoral slogan. The emotive issue was immigration; and on this issue, although Cameron secured some minor concessions, they did not seem sufficient to ensure that it would be radically curbed. So Cameron was successful on a battlefield that proved not to matter in the referendum campaign.

Cameron hoped that the referendum would finally resolve and settle the European issue once and for all, as Harold Wilson had hoped in 1975. But the 2016 referendum has had quite the opposite effect, exacerbating the conflict between Europhiles and Eurosceptics, who now appear more polarised than ever. Nevertheless, Cameron's speech marked a turning point in British relations with the European Union. Since 1975, British governments had succeeded in riding the twin horses of E.U. membership and domestic Euroscepticism. They appreciated that the

British people did not have the same sentiments of brotherhood towards the Continent as they had towards, for example, Australians, Canadians, and New Zealanders. But governments believed that membership had brought great benefits. They sought, therefore, to keep Britain inside the European Union but to secure exemptions and opt-outs from integrationist policies which they believed were unsuitable for Britain and not acceptable to the British public. In this they largely succeeded. They had secured exemptions not only from the eurozone but also from the Schengen Agreement, which abolished internal border checks within the European Union starting in March 2006. They had secured a budget rebate in 1984, and David Cameron obtained a settlement ensuring that the rights of the City could not be undermined by the eurozone majority of member states. The 2016 referendum, however, was to show that the balancing act which had reconciled E.U. membership with the constraints of domestic Euroscepticism could no longer be sustained.

For in the 2016 referendum, the dog that had failed to bark in 1975 barked very loudly indeed. There was now a populist nationalist movement of the sort that had kept Norway out of the European Community in 1972. That populist movement was UKIP, the United Kingdom Independence Party, led by Nigel Farage, who proved to be a brilliant media communicator. UKIP had won the European Parliament elections in Britain in 2014 with 27 percent of the vote, the first time in British history that a party other than the Conservatives, Labour, or the Liberals had won any national election. In the 2015 general election, UKIP won 12 percent of the vote, although, under Britain's first-past-the-post electoral system, only 1 seat out of the 650 in the House of Commons. The party was to play a leading role in the 2016 referendum.

In 2016, the fear element, which had worked in favour of remaining in 1975, now worked in favour of leaving. There was a greater fear of being dragged into integrationist projects and, above all, a greater fear of uncontrolled immigration than fear of the economic consequences of Brexit. The referendum took place against the background of a million refugees being admitted to Germany and terrorist attacks in Paris and Brussels. Oxford University's Migration Observatory declared that 'In the year or so before the EU referendum ... immigration was consistently named as the most salient issue facing the country, peaking at 56% in September 2015.'[18] These fears were played upon by the Brexiteers, some of whom put forward the blatant falsehoods that the European Union would shortly admit Turkey, that Britain would have no veto over that country's admission, and that consequently 80 million Turks would be able to migrate to Britain. It is only fair to say that there were distortions and exaggerations on both sides in the campaign. But referendums, like general elections, are not academic seminars, nor are they ever likely to be. Nevertheless, fears concerning immigration gave concrete content to the Brexiteers' slogan—take back control. Laws, they said, should be made in Westminster, not in Brussels. Further, deference towards political leaders, a powerful feeling in 1975, which operated on the side of those who wanted Britain to remain in Europe, had now almost disappeared, a consequence in large part of the financial crisis which had also discredited the largely pro-European financial community.

Immigration and sovereignty, then, were the issues that weighed the most with Leave voters—issues of culture rather than economics. Remain voters emphasised the economic dangers that Britain would face from Brexit. Most economists believed that it would be economically disadvantageous, and for Remain voters, economics trumped culture. But for many Leave voters, culture trumped economics. Some were conscious of the economic risks but appeared prepared to take them. Some perhaps felt that they had little to lose, since real wages had not risen in Britain since 2006, the longest period of stagnation since the nineteenth century. The referendum showed a country deeply divided along mutually reinforcing cleavages of geography, culture, and education. It remains deeply divided along these fault lines three years after the referendum. Indeed in Britain, Brexit identity has become far stronger than party identity; for while survey evidence shows that 21 percent have no party identity, only 6 percent have no Brexit identity.

The outcome in 2016 was unexpected by most commentators. It will be seismic in its consequences. Perhaps the only comparable event in the twentieth century is the general election of 1945, when Winston Churchill's Conservatives were unexpectedly defeated by Labour, shortly after victory in Europe had been secured. There is a splendid story, perhaps apocryphal, of an elderly lady in a grand London hotel, saying 'Labour in power? The country will never stand for it.' As in 1945, the referendum could be seen as an insurgency of sorts, and as a victory for working-class power. For around 37 percent of Labour voters, who would normally have followed the advice of their party, did not do so but voted to leave the European Union—though an even larger number of Conservative voters—around 58 percent—refused to follow the advice of *their* party leader and supported Brexit. But it was the large turnout and the support of working-class voters which helped to swing the balance in favour of Brexit. In recent general elections, the working-class vote had seemed to count for little, since many working-class voters live in safe Labour constituencies. Therefore, in Britain's first-past-the-post electoral system, politicians hardly bothered to canvass opinion in these constituencies, concentrating instead on the marginal constituencies where elections were won or lost.

But in the referendum, where every vote counted, there was no such thing as a safe seat. This was one reason, no doubt, for the high turnout—72 percent, the highest since the 1992 general election. Turnout was highest in those areas which voted for Brexit, while the lowest turnouts were amongst Remain voters. Of the four regions with the lowest turnouts, three were Remain areas—Northern Ireland, which had the lowest turnout of all; Scotland, with the second lowest turnout; and London—although, ironically, it was voters in these areas who were most insistent in demanding a second referendum, once the outcome was known. Indeed, after the referendum, the elites sometimes seemed to be taking the view, not that the European Union had forfeited the confidence of the British people, but that the people had forfeited the confidence of the European Union and would have to struggle to regain it. They might have borne in mind Bertolt Brecht's poem 'Die Losung'— The Solution—written after the East German uprising of 1953. Brecht cited a leaflet by the secretary of the Writers Union in East Germany stating that the people had forfeited the confidence of the government and could only win it back by redoubled efforts. 'Would it not be easier in that case,' Brecht asked, 'for the government to dissolve the people and elect another?'

The 2016 referendum was in fact an emphatic repudiation not only of the government but of the political class as a whole. All three major political parties favoured remaining, as did the nationalist parties in the non-English parts of the United Kingdom. In the 1970s, as we have seen, Edward Heath had taken the British establishment into Europe; but it had taken Harold Wilson's referendum to take the British people into Europe. Now, it appeared that while the British establishment remained in Europe, the British people did not.

The government having been repudiated, David Cameron resigned. The referendum had become a recall. He was replaced by the home secretary, Theresa May, also a Remainer, but one committed to carrying out the referendum verdict in favour of Brexit.

An academic colleague at King's College, London, the professor of European law Takis Tridimas, declared at a seminar at King's, held shortly after the Brexit referendum, that the referendum in 2016 was the most significant constitutional event in Britain since the Restoration in 1660. For it showed, or perhaps confirmed, that on the issue of Europe, the sovereignty of the people trumped the sovereignty of Parliament. Admittedly, the European Union Referendum Act in 2015 had provided that the 2016 referendum should be advisory and it was not legally binding on the government. Nevertheless, the government had agreed in advance to be bound by the result, and the outcome, even though the majority for Brexit was narrow, was regarded by most MPs as decisive. But it meant that the Commons would be required, for the first time in its history, to follow a policy to which the vast majority of its members were opposed, since around three-quarters of MPs had been Remainers. Only 156 MPs out of 650 campaigned for a Leave vote in the 2016 referendum, but 401 of the 650 constituencies supported it. The majority in Theresa May's Cabinet had also been Remainers, as were the vast majority of members of the House of Lords. The sovereignty of Parliament was now to be constrained—not legally, but for all practical purposes—not by Brussels but by the people.

The high turnout in the referendum was a striking illustration of democratic commitment on the part of the least fortunate in British society. The greatest threat to democracy, after all, is an inert electorate, one that has ceased to think about public issues. John Stuart Mill wrote that 'as we do not learn to read or write, to ride or swim, by being merely told how to do it, but by doing it, so it is only by practising popular government on a limited scale that the people will ever learn how to exercise it on a larger.'[19] We learn about democracy not by reading books about it but by participating in making decisions. Nevertheless, the outcome of the referendum confirmed the doubts which many modern liberals feel concerning the doctrine of the sovereignty of the people. These doubts had been expressed much earlier, in 1974, by Jean Rey, a former president of the European Commission who had deplored the coming referendum. 'A referendum on this matter consists of consulting people who don't know the problems instead of consulting people who know them. I would deplore a situation in which the policy of this great country should be left to housewives. It should be decided instead by trained and informed people.'[20] Modern liberals find themselves in curious alliance with nineteenth-century conservatives who opposed the extension of the franchise, arguing that the people were ill-educated, too prone to be moved by demagogues, and unable to understand complex political issues. Some have come ruefully to sympathise with the great French reactionary and opponent of the French Revolution, Joseph de Maistre, who wrote: 'The principle of the sovereignty of the people is so dangerous that, even if it were true, it would be necessary to conceal it.'[21]

As well as a repudiation of the political class, the referendum vote was a cry of rage by those who saw themselves as the victims of globalisation; it was the revenge of the betrayed. They sought protection against the excesses of globalisation, of which the European Union's internal market was a symbol. They sought protection against market forces which, so they believed, were costing them their jobs and holding down their wages. The referendum vote for Brexit was a popular protest against globalisation. But, by a terrible irony, Brexit is likely to strengthen the forces of globalisation, not weaken them. Indeed, most of the leaders of the Brexit campaign, other than UKIP, were Conservatives of the Right who, while agreeing that E.U. immigration should be restricted, had an entirely different agenda. They sought Brexit for neoliberal reasons, to ensure a more effective operation of the market economy, freed from the constraints of the European Union and from the restrictions of Jacques Delors's social Europe. They agreed with Margaret Thatcher that the European Union would prevent Britain benefiting from the market economy. They believed that a Britain free of E.U. regulations and restrictions could be a powerful global trading force like Hong Kong or Singapore. They hoped to make London a kind of Singapore-on-Thames. What they opposed was not globalisation but social protection.

It is this economically liberal view of most of the Brexit leaders, rather than the populist view of most of the Brexit voters, which is more likely to prevail when Britain leaves the European Union. Indeed, it is the view which *must* prevail if Britain is to survive economically after Brexit. For economic success outside the European Union requires Britain to become more competitive by opening up markets and embracing free trade. It means encouraging enterprise by lowering corporation tax and perhaps personal taxation as well. These reductions in taxation can be financed only by reducing public expenditure. That will put further pressure on social and welfare programs already reeling from years of austerity. It will mean a radical shrinking of the state, which is likely to disadvantage the very voters who believed that Brexit would protect them from the excesses of globalisation. Far from gaining shelter from world economic forces, they will find themselves even more exposed to them. They will have to sink or swim in the harsher economic climate in which post-Brexit Britain will find itself.

Brexit, therefore, will lead to a Britain more, not less, exposed to the forces of globalisation. It will prove to be the revenge of Margaret Thatcher from beyond the grave.

One writer, giving the highly prestigious series of Reith lectures on the BBC in the early 1970s, gave them the title *Journey to an Unknown Destination*.[22] The destination is still unknown. But whatever the destination, Britain will not be travelling towards it. The nation has decided that it is not part of that 'destiny shared in common' of which the French foreign minister Robert Schuman had spoke in 1950. Britain had probably never been part of it. In a poll in 2016, the British came twenty-eighth out of the twenty-eight member states in terms of identifying themselves as Europeans. Nearly two-thirds of British respondents did not identify as Europeans—compared with an average of just 38 percent in the European Union as a whole. The only countries approaching Britain's low level of identification with Europe were Greece and Cyprus, which had suffered serious financial crises in recent years.[23]

Europe, therefore, gave rise to a deep conflict between the claims of economics, which seemed to point to continued membership, and the sentiments of nationhood, which pointed to Brexit. It is perhaps not wholly surprising that the sentiment of nationhood triumphed. But the issues of Europe and Brexit have created unparalleled turbulence in British politics, turbulence that has by no means come to an end. For achieving Brexit is by no means a simple process. It has involved complex treaty negotiations and a conflict between government and the House of Commons, which three times rejected the deal negotiated by the government with the European Union, the first time that Parliament had rejected a treaty since 1864. It is, therefore, an understatement to state that Brexit has proved a complex process. And the issue has divided families and friends for a longer period than any political issue since the conflict over appeasement in the 1930s.

Nevertheless, the process of Brexit has not shaken the foundations of the British political system. Whatever the final outcome, Britain will remain a stable democracy, one of the most stable indeed in the world; and its constitutional and political structures will retain their solidity.

In 1777, following General Burgoyne's surrender to the Americans at Saratoga, a young British aristocrat said to Adam Smith, 'This will be the ruin of the nation.' 'Young man,' Smith replied, 'there is a great deal of ruin in a nation.' Those were wise words and well worth remembering amidst the tumult which Brexit has caused.

4

Never Closer Union
Europe Without Britain

Brexit poses a challenge for the European Union. It is, after all, a blow to an international organisation when one of its largest and most powerful members decides that it wishes to leave, and it challenges the standard E.U. narrative of ever closer union. Brexit threatens what might be called the ideology of the European Union. But is Brexit a peculiarly British aberration? Or does it rather reflect anxieties which are also held elsewhere, in other member states? Some of the leaders of the European Union have made it clear that they do not regard Brexit as a peculiarly British aberration. At Bratislava in September 2016, Donald Tusk, president of the European Council, declared, 'It would be a fatal error to assume that the negative result in the UK referendum represents a specifically British issue; that British euroscepticism is a symptom of political aberration or merely a cynical game of populists exploiting social frustrations. . . . The Brexit vote is a desperate attempt to answer the questions that millions of Europeans ask themselves daily. . . . Questions about the guarantees of security of the citizens and their territory, questions about the protection of their interests, cultural heritage and way of life.

These are questions we would have to face even if the UK had voted to remain.'

President Emmanuel Macron of France was candid enough to admit, in a broadcast on the BBC in early 2017, that the anxieties that led to Brexit were also present in many other European countries. Indeed, he went on to say that, if a referendum were to be held in France on that country's continued membership, he could not guarantee that the outcome would be positive. Other European leaders must surely concede that some of the anti-Europe sentiment is not exclusively British but is present across Europe as a whole. From that point of view, Brexit should be regarded not as a peculiarly British aberration, but as a symptom of wider problems and tensions faced by the whole European Union. Indeed, recent crises over the euro and migration have revealed grave weaknesses in the structure of the European Union, sometimes summed up in the term 'democratic deficit.'

But what kind of organisation is the European Union, and how will it develop after Brexit? It is not easy to understand the European Union. Indeed, Madeleine Albright, U.S. secretary of state under Bill Clinton, once said, 'to understand Europe you have to be a genius or French.'[1] I am neither. Nevertheless, I will do my best to try to understand.

The European Union is, like the United States, what the Italian political scientist Sergio Fabbrini calls a compound democracy, a political system divided not only territorially, along federal lines, but with a division of powers at the centre— in the United States between the president, Congress, and the Supreme Court, in Europe between the Council, the Commission, the Parliament, and the European Court of Justice. There are, of course, huge differences between the two political systems. The European Union has no army and no police force. Its public expenditure is minimal, comprising just 1.03 percent of the GNP of the member states. Perhaps the European Union would be better compared not with the United States as it is today but with the United States as it was in 1787, when there was no federal income tax, the Senate was not directly elected, and the new nation was distinctly unwilling to project its power upon the world.

There are two fundamental differences between the United States as it is today and the European Union. The first is that the European Union is a free association of states, which explicitly recognises in Article 50 of the treaty, agreed at Lisbon in 2008, the right of secession, a right of which Britain is currently taking advantage. That right of secession is not of course available in the American constitution, and the attempt to secure it led to the Civil War. The second vital difference is that in the European Union, the Commission, which is not directly elected, has the sole power of legislative initiative. There is of course no parallel to the Commission in the United States. In Britain, and countries influenced by the British parliamentary tradition, the power of legislative initiative is seen as a *political* power, to be exercised only by those who are elected, not by officials. In Britain as in Canada, Australia, and New Zealand, there is a fairly strict separation of powers by means of which political power lies in the hands of those elected and accountable to parliament and the people—with, in Britain, the minimal exception of a very small number of ministers in the House of Lords. In countries influenced by the British parliamentary tradition, civil servants, not being elected, are non-partisan career officials. They serve whatever government is chosen by the voters. They cannot make political or legislative decisions. The British find it difficult to understand the Continental conception of the unelected politician or the elected official.

Many years ago, I heard a Conservative MP address a member of the Commission, the late Finn Gundelach, as an official. Mr. Gundelach bristled. I suspect that Jacques Delors would have bristled even more. But the British do not comprehend how an unelected person can enjoy such wide powers as those wielded by Delors. The Commission has admittedly become weaker since the end of Delors's reign, in 1995, for he was the most activist president of the Commission that Europe has known. And there have been attempts to make the Commission accountable. In 2014, there was an effort to give it democratic legitimacy through the so-called *spitzenkandidat*—lead candidate—process. In this process, each party grouping in the European Parliament would nominate its candidate for president of the Commission before the European Parliament elections. Then the party winning the most seats would have the right to appoint its candidate president. The outcome in 2014 was that Jean-Claude Juncker, the lead candidate of the European Peoples Party, the Christian Democrat grouping, became president of the Commission. Yet few in Europe had heard of Juncker before the election, and it is difficult to believe that those who voted for the European Peoples Party were conscious of supporting him for the post of Commission president. In 2019, the European Peoples Party candidate for the presidency was Manfred Weber, leader of the party in the European Parliament since 2014. Few in Europe have heard of him either. But, in the event, Manfred Weber did not become president of the Commission. Instead the post was given to Ursula von der Leyen, the German defence minister, after bargaining between the member states. So the problem of the democratic deficit is unlikely to be resolved by the *spitzenkandidat* method.

The Commission as a whole now needs the approval of the European Parliament before it takes office, and can be dismissed by the Parliament. But the European Parliament does not have the same relationship to the people of Europe that domestic legislatures have to their peoples. Most Europeans continue to give their primary allegiance to the legislatures of the member states, not the European Parliament, whose elections attract only a derisory turnout. They feel represented by their national parliaments, not the European Parliament, whose election campaigns are still run primarily by national parties. The European Parliament is often seen as representing not the European people but the political class, not 'us' but 'them.' It seems remote from those whom it seeks to represent. As for the Commission, it is not only geographically remote, like the Parliament. It is also institutionally remote because it is not chosen by the people of Europe. It is *inherently* remote. Even more than the Parliament, it is seen as part of an alienated superstructure.

This remoteness is inherent in the conception of European integration held by Jean Monnet, its founding father. Monnet was a great man who understood that European unity could not be achieved by good will. That good will needed instead to be embodied in common policies and common institutions. But Monnet exercised his influence from behind the scenes. He never in his life held an elected position. Perhaps this is why he never fully appreciated that political legitimacy is secured primarily by direct election, a principle fundamental to the British conception of parliamentary government. The epigraph to Monnet's memoirs declares, 'We are not forming coalitions between states, but union among people.' The people he had in mind, however, were the elites, who would construct Europe by stealth, using economic means to lock nation-states together. The people as a whole would be almost unaware of the process until it had become irreversible. Monnet hoped to achieve a united Europe without the people noticing. Such a process might have been possible in the more deferential Europe of the 1950s, when the leaders led, the followers followed, and unelected officials enjoyed great prestige. It is hardly possibly in the Europe of today.[2]

Jean Monnet and other founding fathers of European unity actually envisaged the Commission as a provisional government of Europe, and eventually as the real government of Europe, with the European Parliament as a lower house and the Council of Ministers representing the member states as an upper house, much like the German upper house, the Bundesrat, which represents the governments of the various Länder, the states of Germany. Speaking to the European Parliament in November 2010, German chancellor Angela Merkel actually predicted that the Commission would eventually become the government of the European Union. Such an outcome might perhaps have been feasible had the European Union remained an organisation comprising just six closely associated member states, as it was at its founding, in 1958; or if there were to be an inner core of just a few member states prepared to move rapidly forward to political integration, something envisaged by President Macron in a landmark speech charting the way forward for Europe delivered at the Sorbonne in September 2017. But it is utterly implausible in a sprawling European Union of twenty-seven nation-states.

European integration, from the time of the Coal and Steel Community to the European Union agreed at Maastricht in 1992, was developed by elites, with little popular involvement. That was understandable. In the immediate postwar years, there was some distrust of the people, given the experience of mass support for fascism, Nazism, and collaboration. Besides, the aim was to create not merely European institutions but to create, from various national peoples, a European people whose European allegiance would be superimposed upon national allegiances. 'The founding fathers,' President Macron declared in his Sorbonne speech, 'built Europe in isolation of the people, because they were an enlightened vanguard.' But, as he then went on to say, 'European democratic doubt . . . put an end to that chapter. And I think we were wrong to move Europe forward in spite of the people—we must stop being afraid of the people . . . we must simply stop building Europe in isolation from them.'

The institutions of the European Union were constructed in the 1950s, and the structure of the European Coal and Steel Community and of the European Communities, out of which the European Union has grown, was based very much on the ethos of the French Fourth Republic, in which, because of the weakness of the political executive and the instability of successive governments, considerable power accrued to unelected officials. The Commissariat Generale du Plan, formed in 1946, whose first head was Jean Monnet, enjoyed wide powers over the economy and was intended to represent the general interest, as opposed to the partisan interests of politicians. But it was appointed, not elected. Monnet believed that the Commission, which should also be appointed, ought similarly to represent the general interest of Europe rather than the particular interests of the member states. Even today, it is the Commission alone which represents the European Union in World Trade Organisation negotiations. But in France, the Fourth Republic system, in which unelected officials enjoyed so much power, was replaced in 1958 by the strong executive of the Fifth Republic, in which officials became subordinate to elected politicians. The European Union now needs to follow the same course. It needs to confront the problem of the democratic deficit. This can be achieved, as some French Gaullists have suggested, by bringing the Commission under the control of the European Council, which represents the governments of the member states. The power to initiate legislation should be transferred from the Commission to the Council, which would then be seen to be the executive of the European Union. The Commission would become a secretariat of the Council and would lose the power to initiate legislation. Such a reform would help to undermine Euroscepticism, which thrives on the anathema of an unelected legislature, something that Britain in particular has found it difficult to understand or accept.

Angela Merkel, in her Bruges lecture in 2010, as significant in its way as Margaret Thatcher's in 1988, emphasised that there were two methods of European integration. The first was the 'Community method' of automatic supranationalism, what might be called the Monnet or Schuman or Delors method. But that was not the only method. There was also what she called the 'Union method', of coordinated action by national governments. Europe, she insisted, was to be built by both methods and not solely by the Community method, which she believed had been too much emphasised. The German chancellor was giving a salutary warning to the European Union.

The Community method has of course continued, and there has been a gradual deepening of the European Union, for example in financial regulation, telecommunications, climate change, and the harmonisation of drug regulation, although this has often occurred in areas which are hardly noticed by the general public. There has been, all the same, an interweaving and indeed interpenetration of the economic and even the social systems of the member states. Indeed, the difficulties of the Brexit process have shown how difficult it is to disentangle a member state from the European Union after forty-six years of membership. But a delicate balance is needed between the two methods, the supranational and the intergovernmental. If that balance is upset, and supranational policies impinge upon national identities, there will be popular resistance.

The problems aroused by migration and the euro show in graphic form how the European Union can arouse popular resistance if it goes beyond what is acceptable by seeming to challenge the national identity of its member states. In addition, the strong executive action needed to resolve problems such as migration and the euro can be undertaken only by national governments acting in concert, not by supranational institutions. It is for this reason that the eurozone crisis and the migration crisis were confronted primarily by the governments of the member states in the European Council, with the Commission and the European Parliament playing a distinctly secondary role. There is, then, a continual and perhaps creative tension between two Europes—supranational Europe and intergovernmentalist Europe, between an integrated Europe and a Europe that remains a union of sovereign states.

Some have believed that, nevertheless, the European Union was on an unstoppable path towards greater integration, towards the Treaty of Rome's 'ever closer union.' Fear of such integration played an important role in the British referendum campaign of 2016. 'Voting to remain,' one Leave-supporting British Labour MP, Gisela Stuart, declared a couple of months before the vote, 'is not just about staying in the EU as it is today, but also about staying in as it will look in 2025 or 2035.' She was not alone in that belief. There are some in the European Union who share it. In 2015, a report from the Five Presidents of the European Union advocated a much greater degree of integration: the macroeconomic strengthening of monetary union by 2025, a euro-area treasury, and ultimate political union. That, Gisela Stuart insisted, meant 'An EU where the priorities of the Eurozone will gradually and inevitably take over Brussels institutions.' Michael Gove, a leading Conservative Brexiteer and a minister in Theresa May's government from 2017, warned in the 2016 referendum campaign that the European Union 'wants more power over our taxes and our banks.'[3] More recently, the principle of greater integration has come to be endorsed by President Macron in his Sorbonne speech of September 2017, in which he laid out a wide-ranging reform programme for the future of Europe. President Macron believed, as did the Five Presidents, that the eurozone needed to be developed so as to secure a coordinated E.U. economic policy and a common budget under the control of a common minister and subject to parliamentary control at E.U. level. He also advocated convergence on tax and social policies.

These proposals, however, are remote from the political realities. Indeed, the Five Presidents report and the integrationist proposals of President Macron, far from pointing to the future, hark back to the past, to the conception of a supranational Europe held by Jean Monnet and Jacques Delors, who has continued, in retirement, to press for a more integrated Europe. For, despite the rhetoric of ever-closer union, most of the member states are no longer prepared to sacrifice much more of their sovereignty. The Copenhagen criteria for membership laid down in 1993 declared that member states must commit themselves to 'political, economic and monetary union.' But Britain and Denmark had been given an opt-out from the euro at Maastricht in 1992, and Sweden, though not having a legal opt-out, does not intend to join. Nor will all of the central European states wish to join in the near future, even though legally obliged to do so. One senior Polish official has declared privately that Poland was five years away from joining the eurozone and always would be! It has come tacitly to be accepted that the euro is no longer the sole E.U. currency, and it has been confirmed that a member state cannot be discriminated against because it is not in the eurozone. That was a principle which Prime Minister David Cameron insisted upon in his renegotiation with the European Union, and it was readily conceded. Germany, moreover, has no desire for complementing monetary union with fiscal union. There is clearly little appetite for a common migration policy, and anti-E.U. feeling is growing throughout most of the Continent. The European Union has become economically, politically and culturally too diverse for a further drive towards ever closer union to be feasible.

The political integration of separate states is generally a slow process even amongst those who speak the same language, as the history of the United States shows so clearly. The United States, after all, in 1787 was a relatively homogeneous society of immigrants primarily of British extraction, coming from a country from which they had imported their language, beliefs, and values as well as their religion. Its founders had the common experience of the war of independence against Britain. Even so, national integration proved difficult and was not to be accomplished until after the Civil War. Some Americans believe that it has not been fully accomplished even today. Europe, by contrast with the United States, is composed of a multiplicity of independent countries without a common unifying experience, and without a common language or common symbols of loyalty. Nor does union generally occur without a prior act of will, which is often the result of an external threat or is imposed by force—as with the United States in the eighteenth century and the Civil War period, and Germany in the nineteenth century under Bismarck. The European Union is not about to produce such an act of will. A European demos is not about to be created. If it is ever to be created, it will be the outcome of a long historical process, which will almost certainly not be completed in our lifetimes. Therefore the European Union will remain, for the foreseeable future, an association of states committed, as the British Liberal Democrat former MEP and European federalist Andrew Duff has lamented, to 'never closer union.'

The great danger facing the European Union is not, as Brexiteers in Britain feared, that it will become an all-powerful body dictating to the member states, but that its rhetoric drifts too far out of line with the realities. The European Union needs to face reality by accepting that 'ever closer union' is unlikely to occur in the foreseeable future. For as long as that idea remains enshrined as an aim of the European Union, it gives Eurosceptics a handle for criticism. The European Union also needs to face reality on specific policies, in particular freedom of movement, which has become a theology. That principle was first adumbrated before the introduction of the formerly Communist states into the European Union in 2004, an event which totally transformed it. Today freedom of movement not only imposes strains on the more affluent member states, stimulating the growth of the radical right. It also deprives the less affluent member states in central and eastern Europe of their most able and energetic people. Too many of the leaders of the European Union have failed to recognize the stresses and strains caused by uncontrolled immigration. There is no reason why freedom of movement should be in all circumstances absolute. The treaties, it may be said, preclude any interference with freedom of movement as one of the four freedoms. Yet, over thirty years after the Single European Act, the internal market in professional qualifications, for example, remains woefully incomplete. That makes protestations about the absolute nature of freedom of movement sound somewhat odd. In any case, treaties are human constructs. If they stand in the way of reality, they should be revised; and perhaps, even without treaty amendment, it may be possible for the European Union to impose limits on immigration, beyond which the member states could impose controls on the right to work.

In a speech delivered to the Bertelsmann Institute in Berlin in March 2018, the Dutch prime minister, Mark Rutte, called on the European Union to translate its ambitions into practical action. He argued not for more Europe but for better Europe. He called for the European Union's services market to become truly open, pointing out that there were still 5,000 protected professions in the European Union, involving 50 million people,

22 percent of all workers. There was no reason, he believed, why such professions as civil law notaries and architects needed protection. The Dutch prime minister also called for making the digital market and the services market as free as the goods market. Services, after all, made up 70 percent of economic activity in the European Union, and implementing Commission proposals for a single digital market would, Rutte estimated, add 400 billion euros to Europe's GDP. He concluded this part of his speech by echoing Gandhi, who, when asked what he thought of Western civilisation, replied, 'I think it would be a very good idea!' Europeans might give the same answer if asked what they thought of the single market. The European Union, said Rutte, needs to devote more of its energies to improving the lives of Europeans, as it did in the past by providing, for example, for cheaper air fares in Europe. Similar practical reforms would do more than a host of declarations to prove the practical value of the European project.

The Monnet/Schuman/Delors conception of Europe, which was responsible for the early successes of European unity, is now coming to appear moribund. Indeed, as long ago as 1990, when Delors told the European Parliament at Strasbourg that he wanted Europe to become a 'true federation' by the end of the millennium, French president François Mitterrand, watching the speech on television, burst out, 'But that's ridiculous! What's he up to? No one in Europe will ever want that. By playing the extremist, he's going to wreck what's achievable.'[4] There is no concrete intention in Europe to build a federal Europe, except in rhetorical declarations. It is indeed difficult to discover a French, German, or Italian citizen who wishes to submerge his or her country's national identity in Europe. Instead, they seek to pursue their national interests constructively within a cooperative European framework. Perhaps Britain should have done the same.

There is, ironically, a sense in which Gaullist France, as well as Brexit Britain, could be said to have been in the vanguard of European development, rather than hindrances to it. For they both appreciated—Britain thanks to its long evolutionary history, and the Gaullists as a result of France's experiences during the Second World War—what the sacrifice of sovereignty would actually mean in practice. In the 1990s, when Prime Minister John Major, together with other British leaders, declared that Europe was not yet ready for a common currency, his warnings were ignored and he was regarded as an obfuscator. But perhaps the other member states would have done well to have heeded what he said. That would certainly be the view of those young people in the Mediterranean member states who find themselves unemployed as a result of austerity policies necessitated by the exigencies of the common currency. Some member states, especially those which had recently emerged from dictatorships, did not fully appreciate what the sacrifice of sovereignty would mean in practice. It was easy for them to say, rhetorically, that they favoured sacrificing sovereignty. But Germany, when it came to sharing debts, Greece, when it came to budgetary restrictions, and the Visegrád countries of central Europe—the Czech Republic, Hungary, Poland, and Slovakia—when it came to admitting a due quota of Syrian migrants, all found that their acceptance of shared sovereignty was subject to very strict limits. Questions affecting the fundamental national identity of the member states cannot be settled by the qualified majority voting introduced in the Single European Act of 1986 to resolve issues relating to the single market.

The European Union, then, will remain primarily an intergovernmental institution in which the member states dictate the pace of change. 'Now what are the realities of Europe?,' de Gaulle asked in his memoirs. 'What are the pillars on which it can be built? The truth is that these pillars are the states of Europe.'⁵ The European Union will remain what de Gaulle called a '*Europe des états*.' But it will be an intergovernmental organisation with a difference, since member states consider not only their own national interests but the interests of Europe as a whole. The Continent has suffered in the past from the absence of such a transnational perspective. Indeed, had such a perspective been present in 1914—had the states of Europe considered the interests of the Continent as a whole rather than restricting their gaze to their own national ambitions—war would have been avoided. Perhaps, then, it is de Gaulle and not Jean Monnet who should be regarded as the prophet of today's Europe; and perhaps it was for this reason that the great French novelist Andre Malraux declared that de Gaulle was a man of the day before yesterday and the day after tomorrow.[6]

But the European Union not only faces a democratic deficit, it also faces a defence deficit. It is the only one of the world's four major powers—the others being the United States, Russia, and China—which is unable to defend itself but remains reliant upon an outside power, the United States, for its defence. That is a re- markable fact, nearly seventy-five years after the end of the Second World War. In February 1951, shortly after NATO was founded, its first supreme commander, General Eisenhower, allegedly told a friend that, 'If in ten years, all American troops stationed in Europe for national defence purposes have not been returned to the United States, then this whole project [NATO] will have failed.' And he insisted that America 'cannot be a modern Rome guard- ing the frontiers with our legions.'[7] But it seems that, at the sign- ing ceremony of the NATO alliance, the band played George Gershwin's song 'It Ain't Necessarily So'! And today the United States contributes around 72 percent of NATO defence spending.

Europe, therefore, must take greater steps to defend itself. That is the view not only of President Trump; it would almost certainly have been the plea of Hillary Clinton had she been elected, though no doubt she would have phrased the request more politely. Indeed, the view that Europeans are free riders on American charity has been expressed by almost every American president since the war. No matter who is elected to the White House, there will be pressure for Europe to bear more of the costs of its defence. America, moreover, is now becoming more interested in the Asia/Pacific area. That is another development that preceded the election of Donald Trump and is likely to continue after his presidency has ended. There is a strong case, therefore, for NATO to become a two-pillar alliance, which means strengthening the European pillar. But should that European pillar be constructed by the European Union? The European Union has certainly been seeking to expand its role in the area of security and defence. It seeks what it calls strategic autonomy, though it is never very clear precisely what that means. The possibility of such an expanded role was laid out in the Lisbon Treaty of 2008, Article 2A of which called for 'the progressive framing of a common defence policy that might lead to a common defence.' In February 2015, Ursula von der Leyen, the German defence minister, called for a European army, and declared that 'perhaps not my children, but then my grandchildren will experience a United States of Europe.' Her call for a European army was echoed in March 2015 by Jean-Claude Juncker, president of the Commission, who said that a European army would convey to Russia 'that we are serious about defending the values of the EU.'[8] Pressure for an E.U. role in defence has of course been given impetus by the fear that European defence and security may no longer be underpinned by the United States, and that unconditional American support for Europe can no longer be taken for granted.

But the European Union is hardly capable of constructing a European pillar. Indeed the attempt to do so could prove dangerous, since it would be likely to yield high-sounding aspirations which mean little when tested against reality. That was the fate which befell the League of Nations between the wars. It was full of fine phrases in relation to collective security and mutual solidarity. But, when tested by the Italian invasion of Abyssinia in 1935, the League was found wanting. What collective security came to mean in practice was that the two leading members, Britain and France, should use force against aggressors. The others had little to contribute. But in 1935, France was unwilling to act against Mussolini, and Britain refused to act alone. So aggression triumphed, and almost overnight, the League disappeared as a factor of importance in international affairs. It was likewise impotent during the Spanish civil war and Japan's war of aggression against China. It was not invoked during the crisis over Czechoslovakia in 1938; and when war broke out in 1939, it was to be found solemnly considering the standardisation of railway lines in Europe.

A rules-based order needs sanctions if it is to be effective, as Hobbes so well understood. 'Covenants without swords,' he tells us in *Leviathan*, 'are but words and of no strength to secure a man at all.' That was also a lesson which Americans drew from the failure of collective security in the 1930s. Henry Stimson, as President Hoover's secretary of state, seems to have wanted to implement sanctions against Japan following its attack on Manchuria in 1931, but Hoover certainly did not. And perhaps sanctions were not practicable at that time. But Stimson and his disciples certainly drew the lesson that something stronger was needed after 1945 if the postwar world was to enjoy genuine security. It is not clear what sanctions would be attached to an integrated European defence policy.

Britain, which has the world's fifth-largest defence budget and is, with France, a preeminent European contributor to NATO, has always been sceptical of an integrated European defence policy, and with good reason: British leaders believe that such a policy, if effective, would undermine NATO. It would at the very least involve a diversion of energy, energy which would be better applied to strengthening NATO. But the general British view is that it is unlikely to prove effective, that it would yield a wholly fictitious sense of security, as the security offered by the League of Nations turned out to be fictitious. The problem with an integrated European defence policy is that it could in theory require, as the League of Nations did, that a country would be committed to war against the wishes of its own government and parliament; while if military action required unanimity—and currently, decisions on defence and foreign policy do require unanimity in the Council of Ministers—every one of the twenty-seven member states would have a veto, and that would be a guarantee that in the absence of American or British leadership, nothing would be done. Moreover, in the major foreign policy crises of the past two decades—for example, the action in Kosovo and the Iraq war—Europe found itself divided, while today some member states, such as Austria, Cyprus, Hungary, and Italy, find themselves more sympathetic to Russia and China than the vast majority of member states.

The truth is that, for effective defence, the units doing the defending must see their separate interests as subordinated to a common good. That might prove to be the case in Europe at some future date, although one is entitled to be somewhat sceptical. What is clear is that it is not the case today. And this sense of the common good cannot be created artificially by politicians or officials, nor is it to be created simply by calling defence co-ordination a European defence policy. It requires a fundamental allegiance and commitment to a common defence policy.

At first sight, it is cooperation between France and Germany that seems to hold the key to European defence. This cooperation was symbolised by the signing in January 2019 of

the Treaty of Aachen, the city that was the seat of the Caroling-
ian emperor Charlemagne. The Aachen treaty was largely
symbolic, but it did provide for greater economic cooperation
and it also provided for the establishment of a Franco-German
Security Council, with the eventual aim of creating a European
army. Since the time of de Gaulle, who signed a treaty with
Chancellor Konrad Adenauer in January 1963, the Franco-
German relationship has been based on what the French regard
as a complementarity of interests. The French assumed that they
could retain the political leadership of Europe, while Germany
would provide the economic weight sustaining that leadership.

Nevertheless, radical moves towards tighter integration
between France and Germany appear somewhat unlikely, either
in economic policy or in defence. France and Germany find
themselves at odds on the idea of a coordinated economic
policy. The Germans remain adamant that they can accept nothing in the nature of a European budget if that means a transfer
union by means of which Germany is required to subsidise what
it regards as feckless Mediterranean member states when they
get into economic difficulties. In a conflict between further
European integration and sound money, most Germans would
opt for sound money.

More fundamentally, in relation to defence, Germany,
because of its twentieth-century history, can only be a pur-
veyor of soft power. Germany is unlikely to become a major
power in foreign policy and defence in the near future. Not only
has it not reached the NATO target of devoting 2 percent of its
GDP to defence spending, Germany has not even reached its
own target of 1.5 percent. In 2019 German defence spending
was around 1.2 percent. This failure is more worrying than in
the past precisely because the American commitment to Europe
is currently in some doubt. Indeed the Trump administration
has been pressing Germany to be more visible in the defence of

Poland. The Bundestag, the lower house of the German legislature, made objections which prevented a European response to the civil war in Syria, and it was only after a long and anguished debate that Germany agreed to support intervention in Mali in 2013. Moreover, while eight NATO allies took part in intervention in Libya in 2011, Germany restricted itself to naval operations. Constitutional restrictions prevented the Germans from participating in Bosnia in the 1990s, and they are unwilling to join the French initiative for a Euro corps in Africa because it would have too many echoes of Rommel's Afrika Korps.

In 1952, Harold Macmillan had presciently written in his diaries, 'The French are frightened of the Germans; the Germans are frightened of themselves.'[9] A senior British Foreign Office diplomat told me that he had said to his German counterpart, Brexit will make you more powerful than ever. 'Yes,' was the reply, 'but even less willing and less able to use that power.' To the extent that Germany is a hegemonic power in the post-Brexit European Union, it is a reluctant hegemon. In 2011, Polish foreign minister Radek Sikorski said that he feared German power less than he feared German inactivity. A former British ambassador to Berlin has written, 'It is not Germany which has set out to lead: it is others who have chosen to follow.'[10] If there is to be a genuine European defence policy, the key lies not in Berlin but in London.

There is indeed a strong case for NATO to become a two-pillar alliance with a strengthened European pillar. But that pillar must be intergovernmental. A European pillar is hardly possible without Britain, one of two nuclear powers in Europe, and one of just seven out of NATO's twenty-nine member states to meet the 2 percent target. Britain is indeed the second largest spender on defence in the organisation, behind only the United States. European defence must depend primarily upon Britain and upon France, the only other European nuclear power. Together the two countries account for just under half of the European defence budget and capabilities. Theresa May said on a number of occasions that although Britain is leaving the European Union, it is not leaving Europe. For the safety of the nation is, as it has always been, closely bound up with the safety of Europe as a whole, and in particular with the safety of France. In the first half of the twentieth century, a firm alliance between Britain and France might well have prevented both world wars; indeed the failure to cement such an alliance almost cost both countries their national existence.

But if European defence must be intergovernmental, and if it depends primarily upon Britain and France, it cannot be within an E.U. framework, since Britain is leaving the European Union. It must therefore be outside the E.U. framework. In 1944, de Gaulle had believed that there was a need for Anglo-French unity in the postwar world. 'Confronting a new world . . . our two old nations find themselves simultaneously weakened; if they remain divided as well, how much influence will either of them wield. . . . They, England and France, will together create peace, as twice in thirty years they have together confronted war.'[11] Sadly, his own policies when in power after 1958 did little to help secure that unity between the two countries. But he continued to believe that if Europe wanted to be a power in the world, the continent had to develop its own defence arrangements and that these had to be outside what was then the European Community, and also outside NATO. That was the basis of his Fouchet plan in 1962 and of his suggestion in 1969 to the British ambassador, Sir Christopher Soames, that a four-power directorate be established, comprising Britain, France, Germany, and Italy, to manage foreign policy and defence. Such an approach was, of course, quite inconsistent with de Gaulle's view that Britain was not fundamentally a European power; and it is inconsistent with the tradition of the Fifth

Republic, continued to some extent by President Macron, of marginalising Britain as a power in Europe.

France should abandon its strategy of seeing Brexit merely in financial and trade terms, as an opportunity for French business and finance. This strategy is self-defeating if France wants Europe to be a power in the world. The European Union, after all, is not just a means of securing economic growth. Its purpose is also to strengthen Europe in the world. But a strong Europe cannot be built without Britain. So France should appreciate that for a liberal Europe to be able to defend itself, a revival of the entente cordiale is essential. That entente had in effect been abandoned when Britain refused to join the Coal and Steel Community and France instead formed a partnership with Germany. But Germany has never been able to provide the political and diplomatic leadership that could have been given by Britain. A renewal of the entente would not, as is sometimes perceived in the United States, be an attempt to push America out of Europe. Rather it would be strengthening and making more credible the NATO defence commitment.

The European project is currently in some danger. The European Parliament elections of May 2019 brought gains on the Continent for the so-called populist parties such as the Front National in France, the Alternative für Deutschland, the League in Italy, and the Sweden Democrats. The illiberal approach of these parties and their intolerance towards minorities directly contradict the purposes for which the European Union was established. President Macron has declared that the European Union faces an existential struggle with the protagonists of what Hungary's prime minister, Viktor Orbán, proudly calls 'illiberal democracy,' another name, perhaps, for populism. All this too makes Brexit appear as part of a wider European crisis rather than a British aberration. President Macron has now become a leader of liberal Europe against populist Europe, whose headquarters are in Budapest and whose branch offices are in Warsaw and Rome.

But Britain too is part of liberal Europe. Britain brought to Europe the economic liberalism of Margaret Thatcher, who deserves credit for so much of the impetus towards the single market. Although economic liberalism is, as we have seen, in retreat in Britain, the country still retains nevertheless a good deal of its ethos. Brexit, therefore, will weaken economic liberalism in the European Union. As in the 1930s, Britain remains a stronghold of political liberalism. There is a striking absence in Britain of neo-fascist or Islamophobic parties able to win mass support. There is no British equivalent to the Front National, the AfD, or the Swedish Democrats. Britain, therefore, is part of liberal Europe, both economically and politically. So Brexit will shift the balance in the direction of the populists. That is a further and fundamental reason why it is in the interests both of Britain and of the European Union that Britain retain strong ties with the Continent after Brexit and that the entente be recreated. The future of liberalism in Europe depends in no small degree on solidarity between Britain and France after Brexit. Sadly, the British and French do not seem to recognise the importance of such solidarity, and there is currently something of a mésentente between the two countries. But the strength and stability of France and President Macron's success as a leader of liberal Europe are as much in Britain's interest as they are in those of France, just as the success of post-Brexit Britain is also a key French interest. And the survival of a liberal Europe, a democratic Europe based on the rule of law, is also an American interest, as the whole history of the twentieth century shows.

Although most of the populist forces at work in Europe do not at present seek to remove their countries from the European

Union, there is, nevertheless, a very real possibility, greater than it has ever been since the European Communities came into existence in 1958, that the European Union could disintegrate. That would be a tragedy, for Britain, for Europe, and for the world. For the European Union began not as an economic project, and not as a federal project, but as a peace project. It remains a peace project. In 1949, Robert Schuman, speaking at Strasbourg, declared, 'We are carrying out a great experiment, the fulfilment of the same recurrent dream that for ten centuries has revisited the peoples of Europe. Creating between them an organisation putting an end to war and guaranteeing an eternal peace.' The first step, as we have seen, was to lock the economies of France and Germany together, so that the two countries could never go to war again. That aim has long been achieved. In 2018, Frans Timmermans, vice-president of the European Commission and a former Dutch foreign minister, showed his twelve-year-old daughter the anti-tank defences at the frontier with Germany where his grandparents had cheered the Allied bombing of Aachen during the war. He said, 'This is part of a border.' And his daughter looked at him and said, 'Daddy, what is a border?'[12]

Of course, even if the European Union were now to break up, France and Germany would remain securely at peace. But a secure peace has hardly been achieved everywhere in Europe. In particular it has not been achieved in the western Balkans, where ancient hatreds threaten the stability of the region. When Yugoslavia broke up, in 1991, Jacques Poos, Luxembourg's foreign minister, declared, 'It is the hour of Europe. It is not the hour of the Americans.' Yet Europe appeared impotent to prevent the ethnic cleansing of Muslims in Bosnia and Kosovo, the worst crimes that Europe has seen since the Holocaust. It was left to NATO, and primarily Britain and America, to intervene in Kosovo, an intervention which led rapidly to the fall of President Slobodan Milosevic of Serbia, and to Kosovo's independence. The failure of Europe in the 1990s severely damaged its moral credibility.

But in the western Balkans, most of all, warring neighbours need a common home. In that part of Europe, membership of the European Union seems to be the only way in which age-old conflicts can be overcome. That came to me with particular force, and gave me a new perspective on the European Union, when I was asked in 2006 to assist in the drafting of a constitution for Kosovo. Our meetings were held not in Kosovo itself, since those members of the Slav minority in Kosovo who were prepared to participate insisted on meeting in Slavic territory. So we met in Skopje, the capital of what is now Northern Macedonia. I had never before seen such national hatreds on display. The conflict in Kosovo made the quarrel between Unionists and Nationalists in Northern Ireland appear, by contrast, quite manageable.

The breakup of Yugoslavia offers a terrible warning of what could happen in a Europe that is once more broken up into national states. Indeed, one important factor, perhaps the prime factor preventing open warfare between Muslims and Slavs, between Kosovo and Serbia, was the desire of both countries to join the European Union. It was made clear to Serbia that its prospects of membership depended upon establishing a relationship with Kosovo. In 2013, agreements were reached on such matters as bilateral trade, Kosovo's participation in regional initiatives, and the status of the Slav minority in Kosovo. The Enlargement Strategy Report of the European Commission noted that, 'The historic agreement reached by Serbia and Kosovo in April is further proof of the power of the European Union perspective and its role in healing history's deep scars.' In the Balkans, the European Union has become a roof over warring nationalities, as the Austro-Hungarian Empire endeavoured to be in the years before 1914. Stability of the

Balkans is of course as important to Britain as it is to the Continent. It was, after all, in the Balkans that the great catastrophe of the twentieth century began in 1914, dragging both Britain and eventually the United States also into war.

The founding fathers of the European movement sought not only to create a European union but to recreate a European civilisation that had been shattered by two world wars. What, therefore, was to be defended in Europe was not only a territory but a civilisation, a liberal civilisation whose potential was destroyed in 1914, but a civilisation that can now be recreated following the fall of Communism in Europe in 1989–90. The re-creation of a European civilisation was a prime aim of Winston Churchill's, the prophet of a united Europe though ambivalent as to whether Britain should be part of it. In the House of Commons debate in June 1950 on the Schuman Plan, the plan for a European Coal and Steel Community, Churchill spoke of 'the *revival* of a united Europe as a vast factor in the preserving of what is left of the civilisation and culture of the free world' (emphasis added). In his Albert Hall speech in May 1947, Churchill declared that he had been taught during geography lessons as a child 'that there is a continent called Europe,' and that after living a long time, 'I still believe it is true.' Professional geographers 'now tell us that the Continent of Europe is really on "the peninsula of the Asian land mass." I must tell you in all faith that I feel that would be an arid and uninspiring conclusion.' For 'the real demarcation between Europe and Asia,' he continued, was 'no chain of mountains, no natural frontier, but a system of beliefs and ideas which we call Western civilisation.' De Gaulle had said something similar in 1944, when he declared that Europe could offer primacy 'to a certain conception of man despite the progressive mechanization of society.'[13]

During Churchill's youth, at the end of the nineteenth century, people often spoke of the unity of European civilisation.

Those were the days of the Concert of Europe, a system of diplomacy which proved able, despite the absence of supranational machinery, to resolve international conflicts. The Concert's final achievement was the Treaty of London of 1913, which ended the first Balkan war. The Concert failed, of course, after Sarajevo in 1914, just as Europe was to fail at Sarajevo in 1992.

It was because Churchill understood that Europe was not just a geographical region but a civilisation that he was so strong a supporter of the European Convention on Human Rights. The Convention of course is a product of the Council of Europe, an organisation separate from the European Union. Nevertheless, the 1993 Copenhagen criteria for admission to the European Union prescribe that all member states must observe the rule of law, human rights, and respect for minorities. In the Lisbon Treaty of 2008, the European Union adopted its own Charter of Fundamental Rights, which applies to the legislation of the member states when implementing E.U. law. The Charter is a much more wide-ranging document than the European Convention on Human Rights, providing, amongst other rights, a right to non-discrimination on grounds 'such as sex, race, colour, ethnic or social origin, genetic features, language, religion or belief, political or any other opinion, membership of a national minority, property, birth, disability, age or sexual orientation.' The Charter is binding on all member states, and judges in every member state are required to strike down any legislation implementing E.U. law which conflicts with it.

Of course, the European Union does not always live up to its grand principles. It must in particular do more to ensure that Hungary and Poland observe the rule of law. The single market, after all, depends on the rule of law—on trust and the independent arbitration of disputes. If the European Union did a better job of maintaining democratic and human rights standards among its member states, it would have a better chance of inspiring its citizens. Nevertheless, the rule of law is likely to be better protected in a united Europe than in a Europe of nation-states. The illiberal countries of eastern and central Europe would be even more illiberal without the existence of the European Union.

The European Union today is far from Jean Monnet's supranational vision. That Europe, the Europe created by Monnet, the Europe of the 1950s and 1960s, enjoyed a sense of legitimacy derived from postwar idealism and the prestige of the supranational political movements that had been prominent in the resistance—primarily socialism and Christian democracy. But postwar idealism has been dissipated as Europe has struggled to deal with the problems of the eurozone, migration, and terrorism. The European Union now needs to recreate that idealism so as to reestablish an emotional resonance with the people it seeks to represent. Paradoxically, that can best be done by revising the integrationism of the founding fathers and concentrating instead on concrete achievements to improve the lives of Europe's citizens while reforming its institutional machinery so that it better reflects the primacy of national states and the needs of democratic accountability.

I return at the end to Henry Stimson. He was a leading architect of the postwar international order, an order underpinned by American leadership. He and the American statesmen who followed him—men such as Marshall and Acheson—were profoundly conscious of the fragility of international order. They had seen it destroyed not just by one but by two ruinous world wars. The same perception animated those European leaders who sought a united Europe after 1945—men such as Winston Churchill, Konrad Adenauer, and Robert Schuman. International order had broken down in 1914 with the outbreak of the First World War, called by George Kennan the 'seminal catastrophe' of the twentieth century. Before that Europe had known almost a hundred years of peace. Such wars as had occurred did not undermine the framework of European civilisation. People had taken peace for granted, underestimating how fragile was the balance of power which sustained it. Europe could, so some believed in 1914, easily survive a short war directed against a small recalcitrant state such as Serbia. In the words of the great diplomatic historian A.J.P. Taylor, 'All thought that war could be fitted into the existing framework of civilisation. . . . War was expected to interrupt the even tenor of civilian life only while it lasted.' Sir Edward Grey, the British foreign secretary, 'expressed this outlook in extreme form, when he said in the House of Commons on 3 August 1914, "If we are engaged in war, we shall suffer but little more than we shall suffer if we stand aside".' When the Austrian socialist Victor Adler told Austria's foreign minister in 1914 that war would provoke revolution in Russia and perhaps even in the Habsburg empire itself, the foreign minister, Leopold von Berchtold, retorted, 'And who will lead this revolution? Perhaps Mr. Bronstein sitting over there at the Café Central.'[14] Mr. Bronstein turned out to be Leon Trotsky, and he did indeed lead a revolution.

The chain of events which began with the murder of the Austrian archduke in Sarajevo was to encompass almost the whole of the twentieth century, ending only with the collapse of Communism in the Soviet Union in 1991. From the ruins of the Continent after 1945, the founding fathers began the process of European integration. It was constructed by a generation all too conscious of the dangers of a breakdown of international order. But now, as the generation which either endured the Second World War or which understands it as part of its historical memory has disappeared, so also there has disappeared that sense of the fragility of international order which the immediate postwar generation understood so well. Now, as in the years before 1914, there are siren voices saying that the international order would benefit from a shake-up, and that any disturbance to it could be kept well under control—the view of the Austrian leadership and the German General Staff in 1914. They were of course utterly wrong in that belief. Their successors—the leaders of illiberalism in Europe and elsewhere—are equally wrong today. The European Union can help to ensure that they are less successful today than their predecessors were in 1914.

In September 2014, Christine Lagarde, managing director of the International Monetary Fund, told a lunch at the *Financial Times* that she was 'particularly concerned about what she sees as a structural disconnect between economic and political structures.' While the global economic system was becoming increasingly integrated, the global political system was fragmented and becoming more so because of a backlash against globalisation. Lagarde's interlocutor, Gillian Tett, responded that 'this makes for a dangerous cocktail, since it creates a world that is interconnected in the sense that shocks can spread quickly, but nobody is actually in charge.' Lagarde nodded and her playful manner disappeared. 'It is not clear which of these trends will win. I am worried. Very worried. I don't want my children, my grandchildren, to grow up in a world which is disaggregated and fragmented.'[15] The task of Europeans is to prevent our world from becoming a world disaggregated and fragmented into conflicting national or ethnic groups, a world of competing national states. That requires what Robert Schuman, in presenting his plan in 1950, called 'creative efforts proportionate to the dangers which threaten it.' Those creative efforts are just as necessary today.

At the beginning of this book I suggested that while liberals in the nineteenth century had welcomed nationalism, their late twentieth century counterparts had sought to transcend it. In a remarkable valedictory speech to the European Parliament in January 1995, just over a year before his death, French president François Mitterrand spoke of his childhood amidst families torn apart by the First World War who were mourning their dead and nursing a hatred against their traditional enemies. He spoke of his time in a German prison camp in the Second World War. War, he declared, had been Europe's past. But it was not only Europe's past. It could also be Europe's future. And it was up to Europeans to ensure that it was not Europe's future. It was up to Europeans to become the guardians of peace and of security. For nationalism, he concluded, meant war. *'Le nationalisme, c'est la guerre.'*

Appendix A
British Prime Ministers, 1945–2019

1945–1951.	Clement Attlee, Labour
1951–1955.	(Sir) Winston Churchill, Conservative
1955–1957.	Sir Anthony Eden, Conservative
1957–1963.	Harold Macmillan, Conservative
1963–1964.	Sir Alec Douglas-Home, Conservative
1964–1970.	Harold Wilson, Labour
1970–1974.	Edward Heath, Conservative
1974–1976.	Harold Wilson, Labour
1976–1979.	James Callaghan, Labour
1979–1990.	Margaret Thatcher, Conservative
1990–1997.	John Major, Conservative
1997–2007.	Tony Blair, Labour
2007–2010.	Gordon Brown, Labour
2010–2015.	David Cameron, Conservative/Liberal Democrat coalition
2015–2016.	David Cameron, Conservative
2016–2019.	Theresa May, Conservative
2019– .	Boris Johnson, Conservative

Appendix B
British General Elections, 2010–2019

2010

Conservatives — 36 percent; 307 seats
Labour — 29 percent; 258 seats
Liberal Democrats — 23 percent; 57 seats
Scottish National Party — 2 percent; 6 seats
Plaid Cymru (Welsh nationalists) — 1 percent; 3 seats
Greens — 1 percent; 1 seat
Northern Ireland parties — 2 percent; 18 seats
United Kingdom Independence Party — 3 percent; 0 seats
Others — 3 percent; 0 seats
                    Total: 650 seats

2015

Conservatives — 37 percent; 331 seats
Labour — 30 percent; 232 seats
Liberal Democrats — 8 percent; 8 seats
Scottish National Party — 5 percent (50 percent of Scottish vote); 56 seats
Plaid Cymru — 1 percent; 3 seats
United Kingdom Independence Party — 12 percent; 1 seat
Greens — 4 percent; 1 seat
Northern Ireland parties — 2 percent; 18 seats
Others — 1 percent; 0 seats
                    Total: 650 seats

2017

Conservatives — 42 percent; 318 seats
Labour — 40 percent; 262 seats
Liberal Democrats — 7 percent; 12 seats
Scottish National Party — 3 percent (37 percent of Scottish vote); 35 seats
Plaid Cymru — 1 percent; 4 seats
Greens — 2 percent; 1 seat
United Kingdom Independence Party — 2 percent; 0 seats
Northern Ireland parties — 2 percent; 18 seats
Others — 1 percent; 0 seats
                    Total: 650 seats

2019

Conservatives — 44 percent; 365 seats
Labour — 32 percent; 202 seats
Liberal Democrats — 12 percent; 11 seats
Scottish National Party — 4 percent (45 percent of Scottish vote); 48 seats
Plaid Cymru — 1 percent (10 percent of Welsh vote); 4 seats
Greens — 1 percent; 1 seat
Brexit Party — 2 percent; 0 seats
Northern Ireland parties — 2 percent; 18 seats
Others — 2 percent; 1 seat
                    Total: 650 seats

Appendix C
Referendums on Europe

1975

Do You Think that the United Kingdom should stay in the European Community (the Common Market)?

Yes: 67 percent
No: 33 percent
Turnout: 65 percent

2016

Should the United Kingdom remain a member of the European Union or leave the European Union?

Leave: 52 percent
Remain: 48 percent
Turnout: 72 percent

Notes

1
'Reserve, but Proud Reserve'

1. Quoted in John Lukacs, *The Last European War: September 1939/ December 1941*, Routledge and Kegan Paul, 1976, p. 507fn.

2. Quoted in Norman Davies, *White Eagle, Red Star: The Polish-Soviet War, 1919–1920, and 'the Miracle on the Vistula'* (1972), Pimlico, 2003, p. 63.

3. Robert Lansing, *The Peace Negotiations* (1921), cited in Nicholas Mansergh, *The Irish Question, 1840–1921*, 3rd edition, University of Toronto Press, 1975, pp. 302–3.

4. François Duchêne, *Jean Monnet: The First Statesman of Interdependence*, Norton, 1994, p. 181.

5. The title of François Duchêne's biography.

6. House of Commons, 9 April 1975, Hansard vol. 889, col.1277. This was Heath's first speech in the House of Commons after being defeated for the Conservative leadership.

7. Conversation between Peter Hennessy and Lord Franks, 1990, quoted in Hennessy, *Having It So Good: Britain in the Fifties*, Allen Lane, 2006, p. 295.

8. Oliver S. Franks, *Britain and the Ride of World Affairs: The BBC Reith Lectures 1954*, Oxford University Press, 1955, p. 1.

9. Bernard Donoughue and G. W. Jones, *Herbert Morrison: Portrait of a Politician*, Weidenfeld and Nicolson, 1973, p. 481.

10. Speech to Assembly of Council of Europe, 15 August 1950, quoted in Kenneth Waltz, *Foreign Policy and Democratic Politics*, Longmans, 1968, p. 230fn.

11. Alan S. Milward, *The United Kingdom and the European Community*, vol. 1: *The Rise and Fall of a National Strategy, 1945–1963*, Frank Cass, 2002, pp. 71, 54, 67–68.

12. Anthony Eden, *Full Circle,* Cassell, 1960, pp. 36–37.

13. Milward, *Rise and Fall of a National Strategy,* p. 68.

14. From the diary of Kenneth Younger, junior Foreign Office minister, 12 June 1950, quoted in Peter Hennessy, *Never Again: Britain, 1945–1951,* Cape, 1992, p. 397.

15. Milward, *Rise and Fall of a National Strategy,* p. 76.

16. Cited in Duchêne, *Jean Monnet,* pp. 200, 208.

17. Quoted in Edmund Dell, *The Schuman Plan and the British Abdication of Leadership in Europe,* Oxford University Press, 1995, p. 300.

18. Cited in Michael Charlton, *The Price of Victory,* BBC Publications, 1983, pp. 19–20.

19. Churchill to Eden, 18 October 1942, quoted in John Charmley, 'Churchill and the American Alliance,' *Transactions of the Royal Historical Society,* 2001, p. 362.

20. Reminiscences of Sir Anthony Nutting, junior minister at the Foreign Office, 1951–56, in Charlton, *The Price of Victory,* p. 137.

21. Cited in Anthony Montague Browne, *Late Sunset: Memoirs of Winston Churchill's Last Private Secretary,* Cassell, 1995, pp. 273–74.

22. Edward Heath, 'A Eurosceptic? Churchill? Never!' *Independent,* 27 September 1996.

23. A.J.P. Taylor, 'No Snakes in Iceland,' *New York Review of Books,* 25 March 1965.

24. Quoted in Dell, *The Schuman Plan and the British Abdication of Leadership,* p. 199.

25. Charlton, *The Price of Victory,* p. 157.

26. Sneh Mahajan, *British Foreign Policy, 1874–1914: The Role of India,* Routledge, 2002, p. 33.

27. Stephen Wall, *The Official History of Britain and the European Community,* vol. 2: *From Rejection to Referendum, 1963–1975,* Routledge, 2013, p. 406.

28. Quoted by Heather Conley, 'The End of the West: The Once and Future Europe,' *International Affairs,* 2011, p. 982.

29. Franks, *Britain and the Tide of World Affairs,* Oxford University Press, 1955, p. 39.

30. Ibid, p. 6.

31. Peter Hennessy, *The Prime Minister: The Office and Its Holders Since 1945,* Allen Lane: The Penguin Press, 2000, p. 173.

32. Jean Monnet, *Memoirs,* Collins, 1976, p. 305.

33. Quoted in Rachel Reeves, 'Clement Attlee,' in *Half In, Half Out: Prime Ministers on Europe,* ed. Andrew Adonis, Biteback, 2018, p. 20.

34. Quoted in Waltz, *Foreign Policy and Democratic Politics,* pp. 226–27.

35. Milward, *Rise and Fall of a National Strategy,* p. 67.

36. Winston Churchill, *A History of the English-Speaking Peoples*, vol. 4 (1958), Cassell, 1962, p. 304.

37. Robert H. Ferrell, ed., *The Eisenhower Diaries*, Norton, 1981, p. 233.

38. Peter Boyle, 'The "Special Relationship" with Washington,' in *The Foreign Policy of Churchill's Peacetime Administration, 1951–1955*, ed. John W. Young, Leicester University Press, 1988, p. 33.

39. Quoted in John Ramsden, *The Age of Balfour and Baldwin, 1902–1940*, Longman, 1978, p. 376.

40. Lord Boothby, *Boothby: Recollections of a Rebel*, Hutchinson, 1978, pp. 183–84.

41. Montague Browne, *Late Sunset*, pp. 302–3.

42. Reprinted in Sir Nicholas Henderson, *Channels and Tunnels*, Weidenfeld and Nicolson, 1987, p. 143.

43. James Dennison and Noah Carl, *The Ultimate Causes of Brexit: History, Culture, and Geography*, LSE blog, 24 July 2016.

44. Charlton, *The Price of Victory*, p. 166.

45. Quoted in Tom Buchanan, *Europe's Troubled Peace, 1945–2000*, Blackwell, 2006, p. 102.

46. Quinn Slobodian, *Globalists: The End of Empire and the Birth of Neoliberalism*, Harvard University Press, 2018, p. 193.

47. Cited in Piers Brendon in his review of Alistair Horne, *Macmillan*, vol. 2, *New York Times*, 26 November 1989.

48. Dean Acheson, *Present at the Creation*, Norton, 1987, p. 387.

49. House of Commons Debates, 26 November 1956, vol. 561, cols. 38–39.

50. Ibid., 12 February 1959, vol. 500, col. 1381.

51. Franks, *Britain and the Tide of World Affairs*, p. 38.

2

The Pandora's Box and the Trojan Horses

1. Quoted in Roderick Barclay, *Ernest Bevin and the Foreign Office, 1932–1969*, Roderick Barclay, 1975, p. 67.

2. Peter Mangold, *The Almost Impossible Ally: Harold Macmillan and Charles de Gaulle*, I.B. Tauris, 2006, p. 221.

3. Quoted in Keith Alderman, 'Legislating on Maastricht,' *Contemporary Record*, Winter 1993, p. 449.

4. House of Lords Debates, 8 November 1962, vol. 244, col. 412.

5. David Reynolds, 'Security in the New World Order,' *New Statesman*, 29 March–4 April 2019, p. 31.

6. Martin Gilbert, *Never Despair: Winston S. Churchill, 1945–1965*, Heinemann 1988, p. 337.

7. Quoted in Alan S. Milward, *The Rise and Fall of a National Strategy, 1945–1963*, Frank Cass, 2002, p. 86.

8. Harold Macmillan, *Tides of Fortune*, Macmillan, 1969, p. 466.

9. Milward, *Rise and Fall of a National Strategy*, p. 114.

10. Charles de Gaulle, *Memoirs of Hope*, Weidenfeld and Nicolson, 1971, p. 188.

11. Quoted in Luuk van Middelaar, *The Passage to Europe: How a Continent Became a Union*, Yale University Press, 2013, pp. 168, 158.

12. But one former prime minister—Margaret Thatcher—favoured Brexit in her retirement. In 2002 she wrote a book entitled *Statecraft* in which she argued that Britain should leave the European Union.

13. Alastair Horne, *Macmillan, 1957–1986*, Macmillan, 1989, p. 231; Nigel J. Ashton, *Kennedy, Macmillan, and the Cold War: The Irony of Interdependence*, Palgrave Macmillan, 2002, p. 131.

14. Ronald Butt, 'The Common Market and Conservative Party Politics, 1961–62,' *Government and Opposition*, 1969, p. 373.

15. Sergio Fabbrini, *Compound Democracies: Why the United States and Europe are Becoming Similar*, Oxford University Press, 2007.

16. The constitutional problems are discussed in much greater detail in my book *Beyond Brexit: Towards a British Constitution*, Tauris, 2019.

17. Miriam Camps, *Britain and the European Community, 1955–1983*, Oxford University Press, 1964, p. 440.

18. Milward, *Rise and Fall of a National Strategy*, p. 357.

19. Quoted in Nora Beloff, *The General Says No: Britain's Exclusion from Europe*, Penguin, 1963, p. 118.

20. Camps, *Britain and the European Communities*, p. 464.

21. Quoted in Richard Lamb, 'Macmillan and Europe,' in *Harold Macmillan: Aspects of a Political Life*, ed. Richard Aldous and Sabine Lee, Macmillan, 1959, p. 84.

22. Stephen Wall, *The Official History of Britain and the European Community*, vol. 3: *The Tiger Unleashed, 1975–1985*, Routledge, 2019, pp. 337. The 'tiger unleashed' was Margaret Thatcher.

23. Milward, *Rise and Fall of a National Strategy*, p. 476.

24. Ibid., p. 474.

25. Quoted in David Calleo, *Britain's Future*, Hodder and Stoughton, 1968, p. 80.

26. Maurice Vaisse, 'De Gaulle and the British 'Application' to Join the Common Market,' in *Britain's Failure to Enter the European Community, 1961–1963: The Enlargement Negotiations and Crises in European, Atlantic, and Commonwealth Relations*, ed. George Wilkes, Frank Cass, 1997, p. 57.

27. Peter Catterall, ed., *The Macmillan Diaries*, vol. 2: *Prime Minister and After, 1957–1966*, Macmillan, 2011, p. 147.

28. Vaisse, 'De Gaulle and the British 'Application,' p. 64.

29. Mangold, *The Almost Impossible Ally*, p. 186.

30. Alain Peyrefitte, *C'était de Gaulle*, vol. 1: *La France redeveient la France*, Fayard, 1994, p. 333.

31. Mangold, *The Almost Impossible Ally*, p. 221.

32. Ibid., pp. 200, 20.

33. Stephen Wall, *From Rejection to Referendum, 1963–1975*, Routledge, 2013, pp. 470, 482.

34. Cited by Margaret Thatcher in *Statecraft: Strategies for a Changing World*, HarperCollins, 2002, p. 325.

35. Edward Heath, *The Course of My Life: The Autobiography of Edward Heath*, HarperCollins, 1998, p. 456.

36. *Le Monde*, 13–14 January 1963, quoted in Miriam Camps, *Britain and the European Community*, p. 470.

37. Wall, *From Rejection to Referendum*, p. 366.

38. Dominic Sandbrook, *Seasons in the Sun: The Battle for Britain, 1974–1979*, Allen Lane, 2012, p. 332.

39. David Butler and Uwe Kitzinger, *The 1975 Referendum*, Macmillan, 1976, p. 259; R. W. Johnson, *The Politics of Recession*, Macmillan, 1985, p. 158.

40. Sinn Fein has since altered its stance. It is now a pro-European party and has renounced terrorism.

41. Butler and Kitzinger, *The 1975 Referendum*, p. 287.

42. *The Economist*, 14 June 1975, p. 21.

43. John Lahr, *The Diaries of Kenneth Tynan*, Bloomsbury, 2001, p. 248.

44. *The Times*, 28 May 1975.

45. Quoted in Anthony King, *Britain Says Yes: The 1975 Referendum on the Common Market*, American Enterprise Institute, 1977, p. 154.

46. Butler and Kitzinger, *The 1975 Referendum*, p. 280.

47. *News of the World*, 1 June 1975, cited in Butler and Kitzinger, *The 1975 Referendum*, p. 186.

48. Farage has since left UKIP and founded a new party, the Brexit Party, which played a prominent role in the 2019 European Parliament elections, in which it came top of the poll.

49. Philip Goodhart, *Full-Hearted Consent: The Story of the Referendum Campaign and the Campaign for the Referendum*, Davis-Poynter, 1976, p. 181. Interestingly Wilson spoke of our 'partners' in Europe but our 'friends' elsewhere!

50. Butler and Kitzinger, *The 1975 Referendum*, p. 273.

51. David Watt, *Financial Times*, 7 June 1975; *Sunday Times*, 8 June 1975, cited in Butler and Kitzinger, *The 1975 Referendum*, pp. 275, 276. In 1931, the National Government had won a landslide victory in the general election, defeating the opposition Labour Party by a majority of two to one.

52. Anthony King, ed., *British Public Opinion, 1937–2000: The Gallup Polls*, Politico's, 2001, pp. 301–2; Johnson, *The Politics of Recession*, p. 157.

53. Bernard Donoughue, *The Heat of the Kitchen*, Politico's, 2004, p. 180. Donoughue had been head of the Policy Unit in Labour's 1974–79 government.

3

Brexit Means Brexit

1. But Lawson, later Lord Lawson, was later to become a prominent Eurosceptic and campaigned for Brexit in 2016.

2. Margaret Thatcher, *The Downing Street Years* (1993), HarperPress, 2011, p. 553.

3. House of Commons Debates, 13 November 1990, vol. 180, col. 465.

4. Geoffrey Howe, *Conflict of Loyalty*, Macmillan, 1994, p. 692.

5. Philip Stephens, *Politics and the Pound*, Macmillan, 1996, p. 178.

6. Howe, *Conflict of Loyalties*, p. 644, and House of Commons, 30 October 1990, vol. 178, cols. 876–77.

7. Thatcher, *Statecraft*, pp. 320, 410.

8. John Major, *The Autobiography*, HarperCollins, 1999, pp. 268–69.

9. Anthony Seldon, *Major: A Political Life*, Weidenfeld and Nicolson, 1997, p. 311.

10. John Major, *Autobiography*, p. 323.

11. Alan Budd, *Black Wednesday: A Re-Examination of Britain's Experience in the Exchange Rate Mechanism*, Wincott Lecture 2004, Institute of Economic Affairs, 2005, p. 33.

12. House of Commons Debates, 24 September 1992, vol. 212, col. 86.

13. Major, *Autobiography*, p. 312.

14. Adonis, ed., *Half In, Half Out*, p. 221.

15. I owe these figures to Madeleine Sumption, director of the Migration Observatory at Oxford University. But she is not responsible for the use that I have made of them.

16. David Goodhart, *The Road to Somewhere: The Populist Revolt and the Future of Politics*, Hurst, 2017, p. xv.

17. BBC News, 'Migrationwatch UK Petition on Immigration Tops 100,000,' 7 November 2011.

18. 'UK Public Opinion Toward Immigration: Overall Attitudes and Levels of Concern,' 7 June 2018.

19. In Mill's review of 'De Tocqueville on Democracy in America,' *Collected Works*, ed. John M. Robson, vol. 18, *Essays on Politics and Society*, part 1, University of Toronto Press, 1977, p. 63.

20. Quoted in *The Times*, 18 July 1974.

21. Joseph de Maistre, *Oeuvres Complètes*, Lyon, 1884–87, vol. 9, p. 494.

22. Andrew Shonfield, *Journey to an Unknown Destination*, Penguin, 1973.

23. Robert Worcester, Roger Mortimore, Pail Baines, and Mark Gill, *Explaining Cameron's Catastrophe*, Indie, 2017, p. 46; Dennison and Carl, *The Ultimate Causes of Brexit*.

4
Never Closer Union

1. Adonis, ed., *Half In, Half Out*, p. 196.

2. I owe this thought to Luuk van Middelaar. But he is not responsible for the use that I have made of it!

3. *Guardian*, 19 April 2016.

4. Quoted in Luuk van Middelaar, *The Passage to Europe: How a Continent Became a Union*, Yale University Press, 2013, p. 187.

5. De Gaulle, *Memoirs of Hope*, p. 194.

6. Andre Malraux, *Les Chênes qu'on abat*, Gallimard, 1971, p. 166.

7. David Reynolds, 'Security in the New World Order,' *New Statesman*, 29 March–4 April 2019, p. 31.

8. *Deutsche Welle*, 8 March 2015.

9. Peter Catterall, ed., *The Macmillan Diaries: The Cabinet Years, 1950–1957* (2003), Pan Books, 2004, p. 144.

10. Paul Lever, *Berlin Rules*, Tauris, 2017, pp. 26–27.

11. Charles de Gaulle, *Salvation, 1944–1946* (the third volume of de Gaulle's war memoirs), Weidenfeld and Nicolson, 1960, p. 58.

12. *Financial Times*, 19 July 2018.

13. De Gaulle, *Salvation*, p. 59.

14. A.J.P. Taylor, *The Struggle for Mastery in Europe, 1848–1918*, Clarendon Press, 1954, pp. 529–30, xxxiv.

15. *Financial Times*, 12 September 2014.

Index